THE
PSYCHOLOGY
OF
RICHARD III

A CAUTIONARY TALE FOR MODERN LEADERSHIP

MARK LANSDALE

The Book Guild Ltd

First published in Great Britain in 2021 by
The Book Guild Ltd
9 Priory Business Park
Wistow Road, Kibworth
Leicestershire, LE8 0RX
Freephone: 0800 999 2982
www.bookguild.co.uk
Email: info@bookguild.co.uk
Twitter: @bookguild

Typeset in 11pt Minion Pro

Printed and bound in the UK by TJ Books LTD, Padstow, Cornwall

ISBN 978 1913551 933

British Library Cataloguing in Publication Data.
A catalogue record for this book is available from the British Library.

For Susan

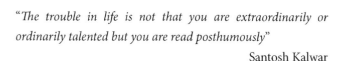

"*The trouble in life is not that you are extraordinarily or ordinarily talented but you are read posthumously*"

Santosh Kalwar

"*In extraordinary times the ordinary takes on a glow and wonder all of its own*"

Mike A. Lancaster

"*Learn the facts… then try on the stories like clothes.*"

John le Carré

Contents

Introduction

In August 2012, Richard III's remains were found under a car park in central Leicester. To be more historically sensitive, they were found in the remains of Greyfriars Priory, where he was buried in the days following his death at Bosworth Field. The discovery, ending as conclusively as it did, confounded the common belief that nothing could or would be found of one of the most well-known monarchs in English history. It therefore attracted huge public interest and, with the subsequent reburial in Leicester Cathedral, some sense of closure[1]. In this sense, there is something of The Parable of the Prodigal Son, where the father says: '*It was fitting to celebrate and be glad, for this your brother was dead and is alive again; was lost and is found*'[2]. In human societies, these closures really matter.

---

1   The story of the search for his body is better told by others who organised and conducted the archaeological dig and the subsequent analysis of the remains. See: *The Bones of A King: Richard III Rediscovered* (2015, Wiley Blackwell) for an account from the Leicester University researchers; and *The Search For Richard III* (2013, Langley and Jones; John Murray) for a personal account from Phillipa Langley.

2   The Gospel according to Luke, 15:31–32.

However, there is another search for Richard that has not closed. If anything, the discovery of his grave has energised it. This search aims to reveal what kind of person Richard actually was. Naturally, all historical figures attract this attention, as do famous contemporaries. There is always an interest in knowing more about the private person behind the public mask. This is particularly marked in Richard's case. We have inherited from history, and in particular from Shakespeare's play *Richard III*, a picture of Richard III as a scheming villain. But the caricature is exaggerated, two-dimensional, and of dubious authenticity. Perhaps he was an unusually unpleasant character, but it is equally likely that his true character has been buried under centuries of calumny going back to the first years of the Tudor dynasty. Whatever the truth, there is a wide gap between the cartoon character handed down to us by history and any sense of the nuances of personality we expect to see in any human being.

Predictably, this received wisdom of Richard's wickedness produces a reaction based on the simple presumption that no one could be *that* bad. Indeed, in a sense, we have known for centuries that he was not: historians were always aware that Shakespeare's play is full of murders that Richard did not commit. Hence, moving closer to the present, the enduring popularity of novels such as Tey's *The Daughter of Time* (1951), and books such as Carson's *Richard III: The Maligned King* (2008) and Potter's *Good King Richard?* (1983). The revisionary movement is also well organised. The Richard III Society dates back to 1924 and has a large international membership that is active in organising events and other activities.

This search for a fuller, more informed picture of Richard hosts a spectrum of attitudes. When motivated by scholarship, it aims to cut through the distortions of popular historical narrative to a more rounded understanding of the man beneath, whatever that might reveal. Some books, including Horrox's *Richard III: A Study of Service* (1989) or Ross's *Richard III* (1981), represent high points of scholarship. Others, however well written, can be questioned. For example, Kendall's *Richard the Third* (1955) is obviously well-informed and very readable, but at the same time is clearly sympathetic to the central character and more than willing to speculate on Richard's mental state without evidence. Others, particularly when enthused by sentimental ideas of restoring the reputation of a victim of propaganda, flirt with the boundaries of objectivity.

We can therefore see that the search for Richard III's grave, and the impact of its discovery in the media, fed, and was fed by, an already eager appetite to learn more about him. At first sight, there seems a wide gap between the identification of a specific location for a grave and the search to understand the person who was buried there. Perhaps the very real evidence of mortal remains, with archaeological details of its injuries and signs of a hasty burial, reminded us that this was once, first and foremost, a real man. By this discovery, Richard III turned from an abstract concept into something much more tangible; or at least, someone who could be tangible if we knew more about him.

So we are seeking a man; but of what kind? Can we, in the 21st century, even attempt to understand how Richard, Duke of Gloucester, later King Richard III of England, thought, and why he behaved the way he did? From the outset, we are looking at something quite out of the ordinary. Some of the things he is supposed to have done come immediately to mind the moment he is mentioned: why did he summarily condemn and execute his supposed ally Hastings? Did he have the princes in the tower killed? And, if so, what would that say for our understanding of him? Historians believe that further research can answer only some of these questions. There is general agreement that the historical record of Richard's time is thin. Some historians have voiced doubt, for example, as to the fate of the princes and whether this mystery will ever be resolved by the discovery of new evidence. But this is not the concern here. This book does not undertake or re-evaluate historical analysis. Instead it asks different questions: can a psychological analysis tell us anything new; and can it add value in other ways to historical analysis?

Before launching into that analysis in the following chapters, some introductory remarks are necessary. They will help to explain why this book is structured in the way it is. Historians sometimes refer to the application of psychological ideas to historical figures and events as *psychohistory*, and their response can often be unenthusiastic. In this case, for example, they will be concerned about whether psychologists are sufficiently sensitive to, and understanding of, the context and attitudes of the 15th century. I share their concerns. Bridging academic disciplines is something of an intellectual minefield, and psychologists have not always done this as carefully or sensitively as they might. However, neither have historians when speculating on the psychology of historical figures. A reappraisal of the opportunities of psychohistory is therefore overdue on both sides and I return to this issue in the final chapter. Before that, the aim of this book must be to see whether this minefield can be navigated at all. The objective is to demonstrate, by proof of concept, that the psychological profiling of an historical figure is an interesting and useful thing to do.

An incidental, but necessary, aim of this book is to make psychological science available to a wider audience: it would not be possible to establish the credentials of psychohistory if the psychology being applied is not itself intelligible. In this respect, it is not unfair to say that the public at large has a skewed perception of psychology as a scientific discipline. To give a trivial example: it will surprise some readers to know that the theories of Sigmund Freud – the first and most prominent psychologist a layperson is likely to think of – are as likely to be taught in a department of English, art or drama as in a department of psychology; at least in the United Kingdom. It points to a worrying disconnect between what trained psychologists think is important for students to know and what the public expects. Academic psychologists – or at least a significant proportion of them – worry about this a great deal, and are constantly seeking to redefine what psychology is and whether the discipline is pursuing and disseminating knowledge in an appropriate way. To give a simple example, one of the 20th century's more influential psychologists, Ulric Neisser, once confronted a conference on human memory with what he called *Neisser's Law*. This stated that: '*if X is an important or interesting topic in* [the study of human[3]] *memory, psychologists have hardly ever studied X*'. Whether he was fair to say such a thing was irrelevant; although I am inclined, on balance, to agree with him. His aim was to make us question the boundaries of our research. One way of doing this, he argued, was to apply our discipline to real-world issues of general interest and then to make a comprehensible connection between everyday experience of this issue and the more obscure realm of psychological theory. If (as he suspected) this would make us revise our theoretical ideas to make this possible, so much the better. This book is very much in that spirit: it follows that part of the task is to lay out our psychological expertise, such as it is, in an accessible form. Some of this book is therefore given over to basic psychological theory and its background.

The problem is that human beings are rather complex, and it is not always easy to communicate the details of psychological theory for public understanding. Not easy, but nor is it impossible or something we shouldn't attempt. Psychologists working to apply their knowledge in real-world settings sometimes surprise even themselves with how useful a psychological perspective can be, and how receptive clients have been to new ideas that follow. I am therefore optimistic that this book demonstrates a range of psychological perspectives on the life of Richard that readers will find new, illuminating, and, furthermore, highly applicable to life in the 21st century. The psychology of Richard's life has an enduring relevance to the present.

This book can therefore be seen as a case study in

---

3   I have inserted the bracketed text to make Neisser's intentions clearer here. He was addressing an audience of researchers in human memory who would have known what he meant.

psychohistory and as a vehicle for promoting psychological science to a wider audience. Achieving this requires a coherent psychological narrative of Richard's life that both makes sense to us in the 21st century whilst remaining respectful of an understanding of 15th-century life. If the archaeological dig and the circumstances of his injuries and burial offered us a glimpse of Richard's humanity, the further purpose here is to understand better the relationships between the context of the historical flow of events and his personal circumstances to identify behaviours and motivations we can understand in the present. Here, of course, lies the crux of debate in psychohistory: can that relevance be established from the position of a 21st-century psychologist? Can a psychological perspective cast new light upon an historical figure?

As a psychologist, you would expect me to say that it can from the outset. But the issue is just not that simple. In fact, it is so controversial a proposition amongst both historians and psychologists that some of their concerns need to be confronted immediately. For one thing, psychological science is grounded in observation and measurement. This is not possible for long-dead figures such as Richard III. Nor were the tools or the observational rigour, routinely in use today, available in his time. Therefore, the observations that are passed down through documentary history have little or no validity as scientific data. So much is obvious, and you might wonder where evidence is to be found: more than one historian commenting on earlier versions of this book has felt the need to comment that you cannot psychoanalyse bones. Allowing this remark to pass for the moment, the point has to be conceded that this approach must therefore involve some element of conjecture. Notwithstanding the fact that they do it all the time, speculation is officially an anathema to historians and psychologists alike, so there can be no surprise that academics are often concerned about the validity of psychohistorical projects such as this.

It would therefore be a mistake to think that the aim

of this book is to establish new 'facts' about Richard III: we must remember that what we did not know before, we cannot know for sure now. However, it does *not* follow from this that psychohistorical analysis should not be attempted, and the purpose of this book is to demonstrate why it should. Rather, these remarks are cautionary: they are there to remind us of the care needed to avoid the obvious and not-so-obvious pitfalls ahead.

With this caveat in mind, this book is based upon four premises that are examined in greater detail in the following chapters and whose purpose is to provide a foundation upon which a psychological profile can stand. These are:

We must seek the simplest and *most likely* explanations for Richard's behaviour. This means that, as a human being, we must assume that he was psychologically ordinary. The word *ordinary* is used in the sense that he was endowed with the same cognitive facilities as all other human beings. The key point here is that this is an evidence-based approach which avoids presuming Richard was some kind of pathological monster until it becomes an unavoidable conclusion. If we can demonstrate that his behaviour was consistent with what we would expect from modern psychological views of what is 'normal', then there is no need – indeed, it is downright misleading – to explore explanations based upon any presumption of mental abnormality because there is no evidence for it. On the other hand, if we cannot explain his behaviour in terms of normal psychological processes, and/or if there is additional evidence for abnormality, then we can be more confident in any claims of that nature being made;

We must assume that human psychology has not changed since Richard III's time. This is a question of establishing that the benchmarks for behaviour established from modern theory apply equally to the 15th century. In a later chapter, this book establishes that there is no reason to believe that, over the elapsed 500 years, the psychological facilities of human beings have changed or evolved in any *significant* way. At this level of analysis, Richard III shares the same psychological capacity and potential as ourselves. Put another way, if the infant Richard was somehow translated in time to grow up in the 21st century, we would not be able to distinguish him as qualitatively different from anyone else; above and beyond the individual differences we observe between all people, whether of the 21st century or the 15th century. There may be an issue as to whether the balance of those individual differences in society differed between those centuries, but this is a secondary argument to which we can return.

We must be sensitive to the historical context of the 15th century. The *expression* of human thought and behaviour is bound to the specific context of society in which an individual is placed. In other words, the beliefs and societal structure of a given time and place influence the way people reason and behave. Thus, to use a present-day comparison, native Australians think very differently about space and time than do Europeans. Such comparisons are meat and drink to anthropologists, but for an historical setting, we have to ask how far we can take the argument that any differences we observe between behaviour in 15th-century Britain and 21st-century Britain can be attributed solely to variations in context. Put another way, this is asking how much our understanding of psychology in the present can be usefully abstracted to the context of the 15th century to explain behaviour at the time.

These are the first three. They are on relatively safe ground in the sense that there are established psychological arguments which can be used to underpin each of these propositions and structure the debate around them. None of them come without controversy, but the arguments are already well-rehearsed.

However, this book is interested to ask whether psychological expertise can add anything to historical analysis of a powerful individual, and it heralds a fourth premise which moves us out of a psychological comfort zone to something rather more unfamiliar:

We need to be careful how we define 'normal' in a medieval king. The usual study of psychology is about populations of people whose average behaviour is 'normal' and against which extreme behaviour can be called 'abnormal' either by degree (someone might be exceptionally quick of thought or particularly aggressive) or in some absolute sense (as in specific types of brain injury). But in talking about Richard III, we have to introduce a different type of abnormality. Compared to most individuals either at the time or, indeed, in the present, the context of Richard's life was decidedly not normal. He was a medieval royal prince in a mortal clash between families seeking to control the monarchy. Nor is there anything 'usual' about becoming king. This individual is always the most important person in a room to whom everyone defers (at least in public) and who believes that theirs is a God-given status, however they acquired it. Being a royal prince in the 15th century came with some very specific privileges certainly, but also with some very weighty constraints and obligations.

So the questions this book brings to Richard III could be put as: how does such an unusual context interact and play upon the 'ordinary' processes of psychology? Can we use an 'ordinary' or 'normal' view of psychology to understand or explain the behaviour of a particular person in such an unusual situation? And what is it worth when you try? We will return to these questions at the end of the book.

CHAPTER ONE

SETTING THE SCENE:
NATURE AND NURTURE IN ENGLAND, 1452

INTRODUCTION: AN INHERITANCE
OF FEUDALISM AND CONFLICT

Richard Plantagenet, later Duke of Gloucester and then King Richard III, was born on October 2nd 1452. An obvious starting point is to consider the world he was born into and the people who lived in it. Since it is generally accepted that human beings are the product of both their heredity (that is, the nature they inherit genetically from their biological parents) and their nurture (how their upbringing and environment moulds those characteristics), a good place to start is with what kinds of people Richard's parents – the Duke and Duchess of York, no less – were, and how this family was moulded by the events and the structure of society at the time.

The Duke and Duchess of York were aristocrats of the highest standing in the realm. As well as rich and powerful, both the Duke and the Duchess were of direct royal descent. They were in the inner circle of the most influential families in England. In 1452, the reigning monarch was Henry VI. He had been crowned as an infant in 1422 and spent the next 30 years of his life demonstrating his temperamental unsuitability for the role. By the time of Richard's birth, in the absence of strong leadership, the inevitable jostling for power, influence, and control of the crown had brought the governance of the realm to crisis. Richard was born into a powerful, argumentative family in a time of national emergency.

Even if that were not the case, families of this status were always, to some degree, robustly quarrelsome. In the 15th century, power and wealth lay in the hands of the great landowners. Rents and trade were in direct proportion to the size of their estates. Power and influence would be further extracted by dominant magnates from those families owning smaller estates who would be either cowed by, or allied with, them. In this way, noble families aimed to build affiliations that generated a substantial income with the power to command their tenants and associates. This power included the ability to conscript significant armies. If these were initially intended for the protection of the family's interests, it was inevitable that these armies could also be used to extend them. The use of force between competing families was an ever-present threat. Actions that were little more than banditry were not uncommon. At all levels of the aristocracy, families would therefore be mindful of the need to strengthen their position whilst holding off their predatory neighbours, if necessary by force. It is also reasonable to say that against this background, many inter-family transactions would wear a civil cloak. Acquisitions and the growth of family power might follow royal patronage, inheritance or marriage in an orderly way. However, even here, as we will see in the case of Richard and his brother George, this had the potential for conflict if negotiating the settlement of endowments for an agreed marriage was seen as compromising the interests of another party. Maintaining the pecking order in this society therefore involved some serious pecking, and in such an environment it was dangerous to show signs of timidity or weakness. Aggressive vigilance was the order of the day.

No wonder, then, that competing families eyed each other with a combination of greed and suspicion. In the normal state of affairs, these aggressive tendencies were often (but not always) moderated by royal arbitration when the monarch sat more securely on the throne. Thus, moving forward a few years, when Richard represented Edward IV as Lord of the North, he was frequently called upon to arbitrate disputes between the likes of the Percy and Stanley families and their neighbours. His authority, and the proxy authority of the crown, was strong enough at that time to maintain stability. But in 1452, at the start of Richard's life, the authority of the crown was weaker, and very shortly tensions would erupt as civil war. Principally, this was a battle for the throne between the ruling Lancastrian family and the Yorkists, but in the climate of the times, powerful families could be expected to take the opportunity to pursue their own interests and grievances where they could. So the world for the 15th-century aristocrat was combative. For a parallel, one might look no further than competing mafia families in mid-20th-century America: powerful, ruthless, and often able to conduct their violent business with impunity. In this climate, doing nothing was to risk giving your opponents an advantage: weak or inactive nobles risked being taken advantage of by their rivals and would be less likely to take opportunities when they arose. As a result, their sons would inherit weaker estates and so great families would diminish. Strong houses needed strong, assertive heads.

It is reasonable to assume that the 15th-century aristocracy would have mirrored this violent climate with a tendency towards aggressive and assertive personalities. The argument rests upon applying the logic of evolutionary Darwinism to what we know about the inheritability of personality and the characteristics of 15th-century aristocratic society. The accepted finding, discussed further later in this chapter, is that a significant element of our personality – approximately half – is inherited from our parents. Alongside this, the English aristocracy as a breeding population was small and had been for some time; perhaps, as a crude estimate, a few hundreds. For an elite family such as the Duke of York's, the number of acceptable marriage partners was probably smaller still. No surprise then that, when Richard of Gloucester marries Anne Neville, it is to a relatively close relative of his own mother; and that his brother George marries Anne's sister, Isabel. In such a way, the aristocracy of England had been inbreeding for centuries; as had the aristocracy across Europe. The consequences of this became evident in the royal families of Europe for hundreds of years to come in the recurrent cases of haemophilia or 'Hapsburg Jaw', to give two obvious examples[4].

Inbreeding is often associated with such conspicuous outcomes. But in England in 1452, there is a rather more matter-of-fact psychological consequence of this inbreeding that has received less attention, and which is the subject of this chapter. Essentially, the argument follows that those families emerging as the most successful will show a strong representation of appropriately aggressive and pugilistic personality traits because those traits are most likely to ensure the future well-being of the family and will therefore continue to be passed on through the generations. It is an intriguing thought that the specific conditions of the late medieval aristocratic society – its size, interbreeding, and the incessant competition for power and wealth between families – had the effect of distilling certain personality traits in this cohort of humans so as to define a

---

4   As a carrier of haemophilia, Queen Victoria distributed the condition to many royal families of Europe when her children married into them. Charles V of Spain was one of very many Hapsburgs characterised by a large jaw, lower lip, and an overhanging nose.

quite distinct version of humanity[5]. From that perspective, we can examine theories of personality and its heritability in more detail to come to a conclusion about how this may have manifested itself in Richard as a specific individual. This allows the next chapter to move on to how the specific circumstances of Richard's childhood developed that personality as it emerged in his adult life.

MODERN THEORIES OF PERSONALITY

How do we characterise something as complex as a human personality? The ancient Greeks, whose views influenced science well into the 17th century and beyond, believed people could be categorised into four types – choleric, phlegmatic, sanguine, and melancholic. Choleric personalities were seen as energetic, reactive and irritable; phlegmatism reflected a degree of contentment and inner peace; sanguine types were seen as socially-outgoing and energetic, and melancholic types as inward-looking: quiet but wise. Although these types resonate with current views in many ways, the Greek ideas, being linked to ideas of bodily fluids or humours, did not sustain a defendable theory of personality and fell into disrepute. Nevertheless, like the Greeks, the modern approach to personality has been to attempt

---

5 Actually this argument applies wider than the aristocracy. A similar argument applies to the peasantry who, by dint of being neither socially nor geographically mobile, and being subject to a different but equally compelling set of social constraints, will have selected a different profile of personality traits more appropriate to their station in life. These distinctions would serve to emphasise the social stratification that was seen as the natural order, with social mobility and marriage outside of one's class unthinkable. Nor was this a matter of contention. Aristocrats accepted their superiority because the religious doctrine considered that the different strata of society were a divine creation. To question that was a heresy. Likewise the underclasses would see their status in similar terms. As a result, medieval society did not agonise about the moral foundations of inequality because entitlement and good fortune was God-given.

to codify an individual personality in terms of a small number of fundamental traits whose relative contribution to personality varies between individuals. This is the usual way in which science seeks to explain the complexity and variety of natural phenomena: it seeks to reduce complexity by describing it as the interaction of a (preferably small) number of distinct, fundamental elements that may vary in how strongly they are represented in specific cases. Thus, for example, tastes are defined in terms of five basic dimensions (sweetness, sourness, saltiness, bitterness, and umami); a small number of chemical elements, some of which are rare and others are common, combine and recombine to generate the massive variety of materials to be found in the world; and our entire genetic code is described in terms of the specific sequences of just four nucleotides in the double-helix DNA molecule.

Returning to theories of personality, in the 20th century, psychologists' theories were divided on how many dimensions are needed to characterise personalities. On one hand, minimal models of human personality, such as that proposed by Eysenck[6], concentrated upon just two principal personality traits, *extraversion* and *neuroticism*, of which we will hear more. Other approaches, such as Cattell's[7] 16-factor model, would have many more. Today, perhaps as much for a number of practical reasons rather than any scientific breakthrough, and perhaps mindful that personality tests need to be standardised across a wide range of real-world situations, there is some agreement on five principal personality factors whose relative weighting go to describe the fundamentals of any individual personality in the

---

6   Hans Eysenck (1916–1997). A German-born psychologist who lived in Britain from the 1930s. He did much to innovate research into personality theory and, as might be expected for an energetic trailblazer, experienced much opposition and controversy.

7   Raymond Cattell (1905–1998). A British-born American psychologist who used mathematical approaches in an attempt to produce scientifically derived descriptions of the number and description of traits needed to describe personality.

21st century. There are sometimes referred to as the 'Big Five' and each is seen as a dipole, meaning that individual personalities can vary in degree from showing a very high dominance of this trait to very low. These are:

EXTRAVERSION
Following Eysenck's original proposal, a highly extroverted personality is characterised by words such as: sociable, lively, assertive, dominant, exploratory, and sensation-seeking. Its personality opposite (that is, the other end of the spectrum) might be described as introversion.

NEUROTICISM
Again, following Eysenck, this is characterised by: anxiety, depression, a sense of guilt, moodiness, low self-esteem, and emotionality. The opposite of this might be described as an individual showing high degrees of emotional stability.

We then move to three more dimensions, generally less well-researched, that have been added to the two above:

CONSCIENTIOUSNESS
This dimension is associated with self-efficacy. Individuals scoring high on this trait are organised and reliably thorough. People who score lower on this trait are more likely to be seen as easy-going and careless.

AGREEABLENESS
This trait speaks to individuals in their social context. High scorers in this dimension are motivated to enhance their ability to cooperate and compromise. They show warmth, compassion, and empathy, whereas at the opposite end of the scale, such individuals are antagonistic and tend to be suspicious of others.

Sometimes referred to as *openness to experience*, openness is correlated with attributes we associate with 'thinking out of the box': creativity, imagination, and a willingness to suspend received wisdom to explore new ideas. Low scorers in this dimension might be referred to as closed- or fixed-minded.

For balance, it is worth listing the kind of personality factors that researchers have also proposed that do not make it onto this list. These include: religiosity, Machiavellianism, honesty, seductiveness, thriftiness, conservativeness, masculinity/ femininity, egotism, stubbornness, humour, and thrill-seeking to name but a few. For this reason, some psychologists have referred to personality only defined in terms of the Big Five traits as 'the personality of the stranger'. By this they mean that personality is being reduced only to those crude character traits that can be identified in strangers, warning us that some traits or facets of personality that may only be seen in very specific, personal circumstances are excluded from the Big Five because they cannot be measured in the same way. Thus one of the controversies surrounding psychological theories of personality is whether we value what is easy to measure or measure what we value, which can sometimes be difficult.

We need to digress briefly on the problem of applying science – some of which is controversial in the scientific community – to issues of real-world interest, and how this is communicated in a book such as this. Readers will understand that controversy can undermine the scientific validity of its arguments and weaken any claims made. But controversy, and differences in opinion, are the life-blood of science. Without it, for example, we would still believe that the world is flat and the centre of the universe. This is the dilemma every scientist faces when addressing the world at large and it leads to a dilemma of presentation. On one hand, concern for validity is entirely appropriate. We need to know all sides of an argument. On the other, if the exposition that follows is obscure and equivocal, it can be frustratingly hard to read. Worse, as sometimes happens, it can be vexatious if it appears that the writer is committing to nothing in plain English for fear of having their arguments picked apart. For this reason, I have placed some of these debates, where needed, in Appendices to this book. In this way, these controversies can be fairly aired, but they need not hamper the clarity of the main text. In that spirit, Appendix One considers some of the issues surrounding the theoretical underpinning of the Big Five approach to personality theory.

That digression placed to one side, we also need to deal with specific difficulties in applying the Big Five model of personality to Richard and his contemporaries. This is because the intellectual context is so different between the 15th and 21st centuries, when personality theory was formulated. For example, the factors *agreeableness* and *openness* have to be seen as relative to the value judgements of the time. Warmth, compassion, and empathy are never likely to be high in any 15th-century aristocrat's priorities when they were brought up to be warlike in defending the interests of their family and when there were fewer social constraints upon how they behaved. Even more problematic is that 'openness', by which we mean being creative and imaginative in an intellectual sense, was potentially dangerous in a far less intellectually liberal society. In the extreme, it could invite accusations of heresy if creativity implied any contradiction of religious doctrine. What is regarded as a desirable quality today was censured in the 15th century because knowledge, as it was seen then in terms of the classic writings, belonged to the God and the church. Since God was seen, by definition, as being unable to make mistakes or omissions, knowledge could not easily be questioned nor negotiated by research and innovation, as, for example, Galileo found to his cost. More likely, it would never even occur to most people to even contemplate thinking in that way. The aim of the church was to *preserve* knowledge, not give its ownership away by allowing intellectual debate.

Nevertheless, and with these cautions in mind, we can use the Big Five model as a practical tool to talk about personality and how personality profiles might differ from Richard's time to today. Certainly it has been widely applied and, in that sense, has passed the test of time. Personality tests are very widely used in: the clinical diagnosis of mental disorder, recruitment, training, forensic psychology, and educational interventions to mention a few. This approach is justified in a remark by a pioneer in the field of social psychology – Kurt Lewin[8] – that *'There is nothing so practical as a good theory'*, which comes with the reciprocal understanding that theories that are practically useful can be described as 'good' whereas a theory without a practical application can be dismissed as an 'academic argument'. Perhaps because of this, there is a widespread view amongst scientists that when a theory that is otherwise good has no practical application, it is merely assumed that we haven't found it yet. In history there are good examples of this, such as Boolean Algebra, which found its application in computer science 100 years after its invention. Being practical is therefore not the only criterion of a good theory, but it is being applied here.

How is personality inherited?

The first section of this chapter briefly considered the socio-political climate of the world into which Richard was born – the environmental context in which he was nurtured and which we can expect to have shaped his personality. The other half of the equation is the extent to which his specific personality is genetically inherited from his parents. One of the most interesting developments in this area in recent years has been to bring together modern genetics and personality theory to demonstrate that an element of our personality is inherited

---

8   Kurt Lewin (1890–1947). A German-born psychologist who moved to the USA in 1933 and who is generally credited as founding research into social psychology.

from our parents and transmitted through our genes. Roughly speaking, this heritability is estimated at about 50%, although estimates between traits and between different studies vary a little. Much of this was revealed by observing identical twins reared separately (and for whom any commonality of nurturing can be discounted) to reveal strong correlations of personality traits that cannot be explained by the influence of a common upbringing.

The question of how much of our personality is inherited from our parents raises three issues of background interest when considering a personality profile for Richard III. First, you can ask why personality traits differ between individuals, and between parents and their offspring: why should our personalities be partly governed – but only partly governed – by our genes? How and why is that useful in human survival? Second, as already discussed earlier in this chapter, we can then ask specifically what the consequences of the heritability of personality are for the aristocracy of the 15th century in particular. Is there anything special about those times that favoured specific personality types? Third, what do the answers to these questions mean when we attempt to drill down into the differences between individuals? What does the heritability of personality mean for understanding the contrast and similarities of personality between Richard and, for example, his brothers Edward and George, these being the siblings about whom most is known and recorded? What can it tell us about Richard as an individual?

Dealing first with the biological logic of inheritable personality traits, general principles of Darwinian evolution have it that creatures evolve by a combination of two factors. First, some degree of genetic variation is inherent in the system. Offspring are never exact copies of their parents except in the most primitive of creatures. Second, over generations, the variations in behaviour and appearance that follow are subject to the principle of 'the survival of the fittest'. By 'fittest' we don't necessarily mean strongest, fastest, or most sexually attractive, although these ideas can and do apply. What is meant is that those variations that confer advantages to the individual because of their 'fit' to the environmental context are favoured. Thus in an ice age, an infant bear with a slightly thicker pelt may survive more easily, but in a period of high temperatures it may be a disadvantage. In the first case, the bear is more likely to survive and pass on their genes, and in the second, less so. By increments, therefore, species become more specialised and adapted to their environments and different environments become increasingly populated by distinct creatures operating in different environmental niches. Note also that, by injecting some variability between generations, life maintains the opportunity to adapt to sudden and potentially disastrous events. These events may wipe out most species (as in the case of dinosaurs), but those that do survive are able to evolve and proliferate as they adapt to the new circumstances.

In the case of personality, one might ask how the same process operates and specifically why, for example, traits such as neuroticism should survive at all. How can a trait associated with guilt, anxiety, low self-esteem, and depression contribute positively to the survival of the fittest? Why has this trait not been extinguished as more emotionally stable extroverts dominate the gene pool? The answer seems to be that this trait has proven essential to the adaptability of humans as their environment changes either through migration or external factors such as climate change. As a trait, neuroticism has been characterised as negative, but the caution and anxiety that goes with this trait is also adaptive in that it selects for greater appraisal of risk. To put it another way, you could adapt the well-known saying *'when the going gets tough the tough get going'* to become *'when the going gets riskier, the risk analysts get going'*. Without such restraints, other personality traits such as openness to new experiences and extroversion can only lead to an increase in personal risk and the increased possibility of immediate extinction. Similarly, while openness lays one open to dangerous new experiences, in times where adaptive change is essential (for example, rapid changes in climate), the ability to consider new and creative behaviours is an essential element of adaption.

So it would seem that the profile of personality traits we humans inherit represents a subtle balance in which nature has hedged its bets. On the one hand, we inherit a great deal from our parents, supplemented by how they educate us. This is a conservative element that is best fit to the existing circumstances: insofar as they have survived so far, this represents a 'working system'; a stable basis. On the other, a degree of natural variation builds into the system a capacity for change and adaption. Our insurance, as a species, is that each of these personality traits confers advantages as well as disadvantages. In this way, when the world turns against us, the next generation has the capacity to inherit both the advantages of their predecessors, but also the possibility of adapting to the new circumstances. But at the individual level, this is a lottery. Some individuals, as in the case of highly charismatic personalities, benefit. Others, for example those struggling with highly neurotic personality profiles, can find life difficult.

To summarise, it might seem surprising that psychological concepts such as human personality profiles should be subject to principles of evolutionary biology, but the logic makes sense and is intriguing in its implications. However, we still need to be a little careful. Evolutionary processes mostly (but not always) unfold very slowly, and the evolution of humans has taken place over hundreds of thousands of years. Where does this place our assessment of Richard III living 500 years ago? Could sufficient time have elapsed to mean that in the 21st century our understanding of psychology no longer applies to then? Or has the evolution of human psychology gone so slowly as to mean practically nothing has changed? This is important to all aspects of this book because the question applies to all aspects of psychology that might be used to build a profile of Richard III and not just to the heritability of personality.

The answer seems to be strongly in favour of thinking that evolutionary change in human psychology between 1452 and the present is negligible. Beyond that simple claim, the arguments are interesting but involved, and something of a digression. They are discussed in more depth in Appendix Two.

The qualification to this argument is that the 15th-century aristocracy were likely to inherit personality traits that favoured assertive, aggressive, and acquisitive behaviour. With Henry VI as an obvious exception, the aristocracy of the 15th century do seem to have been in this mould: a risk-taking, combative, and duplicitous lot. Evidently, these personality traits were advantageous to dynastic leaders. Those behaving in that way may ultimately lose their life on the scaffold or in battle, but not before strengthening the power of their families and thereby increasing the likelihood that their genes and personality traits would be passed on to their heirs. Horrox's (1989) study of Richard[9], specifically in reference to his dealings and construction of a power base based upon land ownership, shows him to be typical in this respect. The suggestion is therefore that Richard, alongside most of his contemporaries, inherited a profile of personality traits that were very much of their time and moulded by previous generations of medieval aristocratic society. Thus we might choose to describe any given 15th-century noble as an 'ordinary man of his times', but this is not to say that such a man translated as an infant into the present day would necessarily develop to be recognisably ordinary by 21st-century standards. We could well see him as a disagreeable, antagonistic individual.

So far, this chapter has covered the evolutionary logic of partial inheritance of personality and the specific circumstances of the aristocracy in the 15th century. The third issue, relevant to any assessment of Richard's individuality,

---

9   *Richard III: A Study of Service* R. Horrox (1989) Cambridge University Press, ISBN 0-521-33428-4.

is to ask how our understanding of the inheritance of personality traits can explain the behaviour and individuality of siblings. Heritability implies common traits between siblings because of their genetic inheritance, but it must also be able to explain how and why siblings differ. This is an issue which returns in the next chapter when considering Richard's upbringing because, of course, personalities develop both as a function of genetic predisposition and the nurturing environment. Edward, George, and Richard, as the surviving sons of the Duke of York, appear to have been physically and temperamentally quite different. Edward and George were taller and apparently more handsome than Richard. They were also, by most accounts, more extroverted. Ignoring the very unlikely possibility of Richard having a different father, what does this mean? It turns out that this is not at all surprising. Identical twins raised in a common environment will show similar personality profiles. However, when the same calculations are applied to non-twin siblings, the effect of the common environment appears low. Indeed so low is it that, with the genetic component factored out, the effects of a common environment on siblings is negligible. On this basis, it can even be argued siblings are no more similar in personality type than the similarities expected when matching two random members of the whole population.

So how can I simultaneously argue for genetic influences in personality at the same time as making the claim that siblings are no more similar than random matches? The answer lies in unpacking the apparently harmless phrase '*with the genetic component factored out*' used above to reveal the complications of understanding that arise when we consider the interaction of nature (genetics) and nurture (the environment) in the next chapter. The first, and obvious, element of this is that non-identical siblings have only 50% genetic correspondence on average. Therefore, the likelihood of siblings showing strong trait compliance in purely genetic terms is, in fact, already reduced. Second, in any complex, multidimensional concept such as personality, we need to consider the outcomes of any interactions that may occur between factors. In this case, these could be interactions between inherited traits. It could also mean interactions between those inherited traits and factors in the nurturing environment, as the remainder of this chapter and the next seeks to describe.

As an explanatory term in science, *interaction* can be a slippery concept because it can feel that we are saying that an underlying trait such as extraversion can mean different things in different circumstances, which rather undermines any view of that trait as a stable element of personality. To counter this, I use an extended but simplified analogy between personality and the entertainment of a football game in terms of just one trait of teams: defensiveness. As Figure 1 summarises, the complexities that follow are considerable; making the point that if we were to consider *five* traits, the possibilities for variation become practically endless. Suppose, for the sake of argument, both Arsenal and Benfica are teams rated low in defensiveness (that is, they are teams that favour attack as the best form of defence) and Chelsea and Real Madrid are rated as highly defensive. The 'personality' of any given match is then more predictable when we know who is playing whom. A match between Arsenal and Benfica is likely to be highly entertaining and probably played at a fast pace as both teams look to exploit the openness of the other. In comparison, a match between Chelsea and Real Madrid is more likely to be dull, as both teams wait for the other to attack them. However, the entertainment value of Arsenal, so obvious when playing Benfica, is much less likely to be seen when playing Chelsea as their attack is neutralised by Chelsea's defence. This can be an interesting game, but it is of a different character. The same trait expresses differently in different configurations. When we consider that more traits will actually be in play in a given team (for example, the team formation or the spcific skills of individual players) we can see how the 'personality' of different football matches can differ widely (beyond all the usual randomness) with the interacting profiles of the two teams taking part. This can be true even if those profiles are based upon relatively few constituent traits. On the same basis, returning to the heritability of personality traits, given that there are some differences in the genetic make-up between siblings, we should therefore not be surprised to find them expressed in diverse ways.

HOME SIDE

	Attacking	Defending
Attacking	Entertaining High-scoring Fast game Typical result 4-3	Tense Low-scoring Slow game Typical result 1-1
Defending	Tense Low-scoring Slow game Typical result 1-0	Probably dull Few goals Slow game Typical result 0-0

AWAY SIDE

Figure 1: The typical result of football matches between equally matched teams in terms of how attacking and defensive both sides are.

This is not the only reason for siblings to differ. The next chapter examines a second reason why siblings develop in markedly different ways. This is because variations in nurturing environments are also important interacting factors in the expression of personality. Developmental psychologists have come to realise that common parentage does not mean, for individual children within a family, a common environment. If anything, the reverse is true: the sibling's experiences and interactions with their family are deliberately diversified. The obvious issue here, birth order, turns out to be something of a myth. Apart, possibly, from some specific effects upon a firstborn, there is now some doubt as to whether birth order per se has much effect upon personality at all. More importantly, it appears that families function in such a way as to *increase the influence* of different environments and any different temperamental disposition between siblings. Parents will often focus upon and accentuate the differences between their children ('Eric is the shy one', 'Helena is more athletic') and structure their dealings with the child accordingly. It also seems that extra-familial influences, such as school, perhaps because they come from outside of the home and represent a different type of authority from their parents, have a significant impact upon the child's development.

To summarise, we can provide an outline description of personality, at least crudely, in terms of the Big Five traits. Current research supports the belief that approximately half of this can be accounted for by what we inherit from our parents. Further, the logic of evolutionary biology, as applied to personality theory, suggests that this serves both to select for 'favoured' traits – that is, those that increase the likelihood of the genes being subsequently passed on to the next generation – and to mould particular populations to the specific environments where they are most suited. When we place all this logic against the context of the aristocracy into which Richard was born in 1452, it is reasonable to expect that Richard was genetically predisposed to personality traits that lead to assertive, if not aggressive, behaviour. Historical studies of Richard's career match that expectation. The next chapter is concerned with the development of Richard's personality in his formative years, against this background of a general disposition towards an aggressive, combative personality.

Chapter Two

Richard's formative years: 1452–1464

A chronology of events

Richard Plantagenet was born at Fotheringhay Castle, Northamptonshire, on October 2nd 1452. His was a powerful family. His father, Richard, Duke of York, was a great-grandson of Edward III through both parents, and his mother, Cicely Neville, was herself from a well-connected family claiming royal descent. At the time, Fotheringhay was an administrative centre of the Duchy, and many of Richard's immediate family were buried at the impressive collegiate church there. Richard was not the last child to be born to the Duke and Duchess, but he was the youngest to survive infancy. At the time of his birth, his eldest two brothers, Edward and Edmund (aged about 10 and 9 years) lived in Ludlow, and his eldest sisters (13 and 8) were placed in other noble homes. This left Margaret (6) and George (3) as his immediate cohort of siblings.

It is to be expected that Richard would have seen relatively little of his father, and to a lesser extent, his mother, who would have employed servants to care for and tutor their children. The Duke and Duchess would have come and gone at regular intervals on matters of state and the management of their interests. As it happened, Richard's early years represented a low point in the Duke's fortunes in the tussle for power between his Yorkist faction, of which he was the leader, and the ruling Lancastrians. The Lancastrians were led by the weak and possibly deranged King Henry VI and the anything but weak Queen Margaret of Anjou. The long-running feud for power between these two families can be compared to the vicious infighting of gangster families in 1930s Chicago, and it is inconceivable that the young Richard would have failed to register both this background emnity and a level of collective tension and insecurity punctuated by periods of crisis, success, and disaster.

Even if Richard was not aware of this by the age of seven, he very soon would be. In 1459, possibly seeing Fotheringhay as too vulnerable in an impending civil war, the Duke of York moved his youngest children to Ludlow on the Welsh Marches where Yorkist forces were mustering, and where the young Richard met his elder brothers Edward and Edmund for the first time. At 17 and 16, respectively, they were fighting men in their own right. Over the ensuing months, the Duke planned for the coming fight, and noblemen (with additional troops committed to the Yorkist cause) were arriving with news of events across the kingdom. However, when the Lancastrians eventually approached Ludlow it became clear that elements of York's army had no stomach for a decisive battle. Faced with defections of key troops at the last minute, York chose to retreat, regroup, and fight another day. Riding off north accompanied by his elder sons, the Duke left his Duchess and her younger children, including Richard, behind.

Their capture by the Lancastrians appears to have been comparatively civilised, as York would have expected, even though the Lancastrian army looted the undefended town and castle. The precise circumstances in which the children fell into Lancastrian hands is unclear, but Cicely and her children were placed into the custody of the Duchess of Buckingham for safe-keeping. Additionally, King Henry VI granted the Duchess of York a pension to support herself and her children. Nevertheless they were hostages in a febrile situation. It would have been unclear who had the upper hand and what might happen next, and for long periods in this conflict, neither side was strong enough to treat the other with impunity. In consequence, for as long as the possibility existed that the Yorkists might ultimately prevail, it was unlikely that Cicely and her sons would be threatened. For one thing, there was a general, if not universally observed, agreement that women and minors were protected from violence. Furthermore, any perpetrator of violence might subsequently find themselves answering to the Duke of York. That said, things did not always end well for hostages in the 15th century, and there would have been a palpable sense of danger and loss of freedom for Richard and his immediate family. Any sense of paranoia nurtured by family narrative in Richard's early years was being reinforced by experience.

On this occasion, things seem to have been resolved relatively quickly. While the Yorkists re-gathered their forces, the hostages were transferred in early 1460 to the household of the Archbishop of Canterbury, who was a family relation. By July, the Yorkist faction had recovered enough to march on to London, and then beyond, closing with, and crushing, the Lancastrian army near Northampton. This time it was the King's turn to be captured. By October of that year a triumphant Duke of York re-entered London; this time to claim the crown for himself.

It was not to be. Consistent with the thinking at that time, even York's allies were squeamish about supplanting an anointed and living king, whatever they thought of him and his queen. Despite the fact that the Duke of York had a stronger lineal claim to the throne than Henry VI, he had insufficient support amongst the noble families of England to force the issue. The compromise was to have him declared as heir and protector; effectively controlling the crown. This did not settle matters, however, because Margaret had fled north to assemble another army, and her ability to summon men to the Lancastrian cause remained effective. Moving north to face this new threat late in 1460, the Duke of York was caught with a diminished force and attacked near Pontefract, where he was killed along with his son Edmund and others. The tables had turned yet again, and with an army of Welsh, Scottish, and Yorkshire men of fierce reputation, Margaret advanced south to threaten London. She re-gathered King Henry VI on the way, and swept aside the Earl of Warwick's army at St Albans. By February 1461, London was thrown into panic at the prospect of a northern horde descending upon them. This time, the Duchess of York was able to send her sons, George and Richard, to the safety of the Low Countries in the custody of Philip, Duke of Burgundy.

By April of that year, the tide had turned yet again. Panic or not, London had resisted the threat of Queen Margaret's army, and the delay gave Edward of March (now head of the Yorkist faction) and the Earl of Warwick time to regroup their armies, re-enter London, and once again challenge the Lancastrian army. Retreating north, and pursued by Edward (now proclaiming himself King Edward IV), Queen Margaret's army was destroyed at Towton in what is said to have been one of the most brutal battles in English history. Margaret, Henry VI, and their son Edward fled to Scotland, and for a while the Lancastrian claim looked as if it had been utterly eradicated. Richard and George were therefore able to return to England in greater style than when they left, feted as brothers to the King. In sum, by the time Richard was nine years old he had been captured, held, and released. He had then fled into, and returned from, exile. Not for Richard the cosy and secure childhood aspired to by the developed world in the 21st century.

Most accounts of Richard's life for the next few years record a time of relative tranquillity, although this is largely surmise: the record is very thin and tranquillity hardly seems a suitable description for the mood of the times. At the age of nine, now the Duke of Gloucester and Knight of the Garter, Richard was sent from court to Middleham Castle in Yorkshire to continue his development as a ward of the great kingmaker, Richard Neville,

Earl of Warwick. Whether these, or earlier, years represent the development of Richard from a weakly boy to someone more substantial is also surmise. It is possible that he may have started life as a weakling infant, but little of his physical development is recorded thereafter[10]. However, given that this is a time of training in arms, and that subsequently he was able to conduct himself with good account in battle, we can infer that over the ensuing years any frailty had been replaced with a degree of robustness.

This time also represents a first period of separation and independence from his brother George, now Duke of Clarence, who comes to us through history as a rather self-important and feckless individual. As a result, it is possible that Richard was able to develop more of his own sense of identity and self-esteem during these years. Either way, it is also a period in which he is gradually assimilated into the new King's affairs. This occurs first by proxy – his appointment as Admiral in 1462 cannot have anticipated much effort on his part. But in later roles, such as County Commissioner, he would be expected to make a more active contribution. To repeat, the historical record is thin, but it has been argued that from this stage there was a palpable trend for King Edward IV to favour his brother Richard over George in matters of responsibility. The historical consensus is that, by this time, the dependable and serious elements of Richard's character were apparent, as were the more vain and shallow aspects of George's.

In his twelfth year in 1464, Richard came south to King Edward IV's court, as tensions between the King and Neville (a man used to making and controlling kings) developed. His tutelage in Middleham therefore came to an end and with it, effectively, his childhood. This is a suitable moment to consider

---

10 Much has been made of the words 'Richard liveth yet' penned by a William Worcester in a rhymed history of the York family. While it is possible that this refers to a sickly child whose death seemed imminent, it is a measure of how little there is to go on (see Kendall p28).

how this childhood could have been expected to influence Richard's personality in the years to come.

The previous chapter argues that Richard's genetic inheritance was, by 21st-century standards, biased towards a greater degree of assertiveness and aggression. But that is a characterisation of the entire aristocracy. How typical was Richard of his generation? How did he differ? What are the other factors that contribute to the formation of his personality? This chapter develops the argument that Richard did indeed inherit an assertive personality, but additionally his childhood predisposed him to be more extreme than most along a continuum that we all recognise today and which can be described as an 'aversion to uncertainty' or, put another way, a 'preference for closure'.

What precisely do we mean by *aversion to uncertainty*? Dog trainers will tell you that treating dogs inconsistently is more likely to lead to a stressed, badly-behaved dog. Human beings are no different. On a purely functional level, boring though it might be, routine and certainty in life are relatively safe and stress-free states of being, and most of us aspire to them. Indeed, as we explore in a later chapter, the human cognitive system – the way we actually think – is also geared to translate the uncertain world we live in into something simpler and less stressful to manage. This sidesteps a difficult mental problem of balancing all the pros and cons of risks and opportunities, and thereby allows humans to function when otherwise they could be paralysed by indecision. More generally, risk and threat are aversive stimuli that we avoid where possible. In modern life, some people are exceptions to this, but that is what they are: exceptions. Risk-takers – mountaineers, for example – are more skilled in their chosen field and for them the risks are thereby diminished. Furthermore, following a classic bias of what is called personal agency, they overestimate their own expertise and control over those risks. Hence they are more tolerant of the risks they do perceive, although for them there may also be the reward of taking on and overcoming particular challenges. And we should not forget that a significant number of mountaineers die or are seriously injured as a result. For the rest of us, risk, threat, punishment, and violence are things we learned to avoid in childhood where possible; and if not possible, to develop adaptive strategies to deal with them.

These strategies take many forms. The most moderate are behaviour patterns such as tidiness (to avoid losing things), cleanliness (to avoid catching things), and intellectual rigidity (to avoid making difficult decisions) that emerge as the child moves into adulthood. More extreme, but not uncommon, is a syndrome that earns the title of 'control freak'. This can involve a range of behaviours such as stubbornness, assumptions of roles of dominance, excessive attention to detail, and insensitivity to alternative points of view. More extreme behavioural adaptions to risk and uncertainty border on the socio-pathological. Obsessive-compulsive behaviour such as persistent hand-washing is also seen as having its origins in a desire to impose control and order on life as a response to an early life of uncertainty. If that behaviour is harmless (except possibly for the individual concerned), other extremes are socially aberrant. This could include pathological authoritarianism, where an absolute intolerance to alternative points of view leads to repression, and even genocide when such people who find themselves in positions of power feel threatened. Fortunately, these are uncommon. Most of our responses to control uncertainty and minimise threats, an issue common to us all, emerge in the minutae of ordinary life in descriptions of habit, protectiveness, caution, and parsimony, to name but a few.

Some evidence points to a genetic component for some of these behaviours. But overall, most of this behaviour is a learned response to the child's earlier life. The child may feel insecure, may experience a chaotic childhood, or perhaps is over-criticised or is placed in impossible positions of responsibility where failure is both inevitable and punished. These are all mechanisms that increase the child's overall anxiety, reduce their self-esteem, or cause overcompensation to protect it. Other factors described by psychologists include cases where parents are overly hierarchical, exploitative, or authoritarian, requiring obedience to convention and are preoccupied with social status. In the extreme, the consequent feelings of resentment and aggression, possibly coupled with senses of inferiority or insignificance, can also lead to an aggressive overcompensation in which individuals see the world as totally hostile and lacking in any sense whereby relationships can be mutually supportive. From these extreme beginnings are born the psychopaths and the dangerous authoritarians.

If not extreme, there is no doubt that Richard's childhood involved heightened senses of threat and insecurity. He would have been schooled in the need for self-reliance from his earliest years. He would certainly have been aware of the conflict within which his family was involved because this would have been a matter of routine narrative. His father, mother, elder brothers, and their retinue would have been absent for extended periods and the remaining siblings were regularly moved from castle to castle for their own protection. Aged six, he was left to the mercy of the Lancastrians as his father and elder brothers fled Ludlow. Later, he was forced to flee to the continent to escape Margaret of Anjou's army. In his formative years, Richard would never have been free of a general sense of threat. All of these events and indicators have been shown to correlate with anxiety and corresponding behaviours in adulthood[11].

---

11   The claims about Richard's personality in this book do not rest only on the logic of correlation, the significance of which can be misleading. Correlation does not prove causal relationships. For example, childhood malnutrition is correlated to adult literacy, but that neglect may not inhibit the literacy directly: the common factor is that childhood malnutrition is more likely in situations where education is not valued. Throughout the book I have sought other, converging, lines of evidence to support the arguments made.

We may reasonably wonder at this stage why a very similar childhood for Richard's brother George did *not* produce the same outcome. In comparison to Richard – who for the bulk of his adult life was seen as conscientious, pious, and loyal to his brother Edward IV – George emerges as the opposite: feckless, disloyal, and overtly competitive. How is it possible to claim one outcome for Richard and something different for George? The logic behind that question rests upon two false assumptions: first, that being from the same parents, Richard and George's genetic predispositions were the same; and second, that, sharing the same childhood experiences, the environment in which this genetic stock was matured was the same. Therefore, the logic goes, both nature (i.e. genetic predisposition) and nurture (the childhood experiences) being the same, the outcome should be the same.

Neither assumption is correct. The average genetic commonality of siblings is in any case only about 50% because it is a random mixture of genes inherited from *two* parents, and recent developments in behavioural genetics suggest that the expression of these genes depends critically upon the environment and history of the individual. Also, as discussed in the previous chapter, given the complexity of the interactions between the factors which interact to produce a personality, we should not be surprised to find that relatively small variations in genetic composition and environmental circumstances produce wide variations in the expression of personality. For such reasons, behavioural correlations between siblings are generally rather weaker than might otherwise be expected. This is true even in identical twins raised in the same family, where they share exactly the same genetic profile. To give just one example, most schizophrenic identical twins do not have a co-twin with the same condition. The influences of subtle variations of environment can clearly have radical effects upon the outcome.

In fact, recent research reveals that the family environment, even for two siblings, is rarely comparable: the *effective* environment of two siblings in the same family – that is, those elements of the child's experience that will have an impact upon their personality – is no more alike than would be the environments of any two children taken randomly from different families. This claim seems almost preposterous. How could the experience of sisters brought up in the same Midlands home *not* be more similar in comparison to that of a girl from an inner-city estate in London or another brought up on a ducal estate in Scotland? You might say it is the sort of thing that gives psychology a bad name. Nevertheless, research indicates that it is more correct than any claim you might have expected about the differences in comparing an inner-city London upbringing to an aristocratic childhood in Scotland. The reason is complex because we need to define more carefully what is meant by *experience*. Many obvious parameters, such as birth order (excluding possibly some small effect of being firstborn), turn out to have little detectable impact upon personality either at the time or as predictors of the future. More subtle, hard to quantify factors, such as the *quality* of parental interactions, and, less-studied, sibling and peer-group interactions, probably have a much bigger impact. Above and beyond this, because children only experience the environment *they* grow up in, relative comparisons between a ducal estate and inner-city London are relatively meaningless.

The belief is growing that the effect of families is not to homogenise experience – such that all siblings experience the same nurturing – but the exact reverse. For example, small differences between children ('Asha is the talker of the two') are accentuated precisely because, between siblings, comparison is possible and meaningful. In this way, within families, small differences in behaviour and experience lever larger developmental consequences as the family adapts and widens these initial characterisations. If, therefore, Richard was seen as shorter and weaker than his brother George, who was regarded as tall, handsome, and strong, we can see that two children of similar genetic stock, sharing similar childhood experiences, will grow up quite differently as that comparison is played through, and amplified by, family dynamics over a period of years.

There are many other indications in George and Richard's early lives that encourage us to maintain the profile placed upon Richard while allowing George a completely different trajectory. In this case, although research argues that birth order per se is not a major factor in personality development (despite common belief to the contrary[12]), it has specific consequences in a ducal dynasty simply because George is older. In a family where hierarchy was paramount, George and Richard would both know that the elder is more important in the line of succession. George's superiority over Richard was, in effect, absolute. Other factors might also have reinforced this further in George's mind. He is commonly believed to have been the stronger, healthier child. Also, within Richard's immediate sibling cohort of George and Margaret, claims have been made that Margaret preferred the more charismatic George. It would have been surprising, particularly given what we know of George's character, if Richard was not therefore subjected to some degree of denigration or sidelining. Whether or not this led to bullying cannot be known, but we can be reasonably sure that Richard would have grown up knowing he was the weakest, and least important, member of the Yorkist male line.

Much has been written on the mechanisms by which individuals, and children in particular, protect their self-esteem under this kind of pressure. Freud describes twelve such mechanisms and other psychologists have discussed others. The

_____

12   Many readers may be surprised at this. There may be some specific issues associated with being a first or only child, but otherwise one has to remember that birth order is correlated with many other factors which have far more bearing upon a child's development than whether they are 3rd or 4th in sequence.

truth is that individuals will adopt anything that works, and these lists are therefore merely crude categorisations of a wide set of mechanisms serving a common need. Although interesting, some of these are unknowable in Richard's case. For example, in the *compensation* mechanism, some individuals shift the source of their self-esteem from areas of obvious weakness (a child might be poor at sports) to things at which they excel, such as playing the piano. What activity could have served this purpose in the 15th century is not obvious and we get no historical record of Richard particularly excelling in anything. But then, such remarks would be very unlikely to appear in the historical record and opportunities to excel in various activities were limited. Similarly, in the process of *identification*, some people derive self-esteem by becoming associated with something external to them like a successful football club. All Richard had was the York family itself, and celebrating membership of a family that is attacking your self-esteem hardly seems a plausible displacement mechanism for protecting it. More plausible in Richard's case are various mechanisms based upon rationalising his situation. For example, in *sublimation*, the mechanism works to divert thoughts considered as unacceptable into acceptable attitudes. An intelligent child might argue to themselves that learning to deal with some degree of bullying is an important part of an aristocrat's upbringing[13]. Similarly, in *reaction formation* the individual consciously adopts thoughts opposite to negative thoughts they are repressing in an attempt to protect their self-esteem. Thus, a child who hates his parents (and as a result himself) might give all the appearance of being a loving and caring child. For a child in Richard's circumstances, developing a sense of resilience and self-sufficiency reflects such a mechanism. We should note that the example of sublimation

---

13 But note that my example of 'sublimation' is, in fact, a mechanism which resolves the apparent implausibility of the example I gave for 'identification', demonstrating the rather loose distinction between these different defence mechanisms.

above is perfectly capable of working alongside this, and there is no reason to think Richard did not apply several means by which to protect or enhance his self-esteem. The point here is that there is good reason to think Richard would have had more need of such mechanisms than almost all of the heads of noble families he had to deal with as Warden of the North and King[14], and these would all have a forward trajectory into his adult personality that will have increased his need to control his environment and minimise risks to himself.

Pulling together the threads of this discussion of nature and nurture in the composition of Richard's character, there are indicators here that are developed in the next chapter, which looks at Richard making the full transition to adulthood. The aim is to converge upon a coherent pattern around which we can build a profile for Richard. At this stage we can identify two fundamental aspects. First, by dint of his inheritance alone, any boy born to the Duke of York would be genetically predisposed to personality traits that could be summarised as favouring a 'man of action'. This follows from generations of intermarriage within a relatively small community of senior aristocrats whose families have competed with others for land and power. This would have come with assertive and aggressive traits – possibly with some degree of impulsivity since those traits increase its likelihood. Expressions of neurotic traits would be less marked in this population because self-doubt and nervousness are less-favoured traits in this environment. In Richard's case, and considering the circumstances of his early upbringing, there

---

14 It is interesting to ask how common it was for youngest sons to succeed to the headships of major aristocratic families. Of Richard's contemporary generation of noble gentlemen such as Warwick, Norfolk, Buckingham, Stanley, Percy, and Hastings, how many of them shared similar upbringings? The answer is none: they were all the first or only sons of their fathers, and were therefore significantly less likely to experience the tensions experienced in childhood by Richard as the youngest of his sibling cohort.

are reasons to suspect a second element to his psychological profile based upon a need to protect his self-esteem, not only as a member of the York family as a whole, but also his specific placing at the lowest status in his cohort of siblings. To emerge into adulthood from this effectively, as indeed it appears he did, would require a range of defence mechanisms to deflect the threats and risks he would have sensed from his early years and to provide a sense of control and self-sufficiency. Broadly, I have labelled this as an aversion to uncertainty, and in the next chapter we can look in greater detail at the ways it manifests itself in the adult.

Chapter Three

Adolescence to Maturity: 1464–1483

Chronology

In 1464, his twelfth year, Richard left Middleham to join King Edward IV's court. This move was possibly hastened by Edward's announcement of his marriage to Elizabeth Woodville, which offended Warwick the Kingmaker because it challenged his authority to arrange Edward's marriage himself. It was obviously inappropriate for Richard to remain as Warwick's ward. In any case, Edward may have felt that the time had come to bring Richard into appropriate positions of authority and trust as he moved into adolescence and early adulthood. Edward may also have been calculating the need to keep his brothers Richard and George close and in harness: idle and remote royal princes were useful to those planning discontent and rebellion.

The following years saw Edward IV continuing to establish his own authority as King, and this gave Richard a period of grace to develop and hone his role as the King's brother. But this time was not without risk or threat. Edward was already favouring the Queen's family to such an extent that members of the court, including some of Edward's own affinity, were offended or worse, felt threatened. Not only did some feel strongly that a relatively minor family was being promoted above its natural status (the aristocracy being a highly hierarchical society), but the Woodvilles themselves were seen as highly ambitious. Any dynastic progress on their part could only be at the expense of someone else. To Richard, this background tension presented both specific and indirect threats. A direct threat followed from Richard's high position in the line of succession and the likelihood that others might want either to eliminate him to weaken Edward or use him for their own advantage (but at his own risk). Less directly personal to Richard, the indirect threat was that the court was becoming a more hazardous place with the ever-present possibility of squabbles and resentments within and between noble families. This could easily return to armed conflict, into which Richard would inevitably be dragged. In particular, the unsettled Earl of Warwick was seeing his dominant position undermined. Slowly but inevitably, fault lines were emerging between Warwick, the Woodvilles, and the King. For the King's brothers Richard and George, delicate diplomacy was called for.

Perhaps, given his age and position in the line of succession, Richard was for the while of less interest to other people's schemes. Whatever the reason, he was left to occupy the place of loyal and politically disengaged younger brother. George, on the other hand, became very much engaged, and increasingly associated with Warwick. In so doing, he implicitly placed himself as an alternative to Edward whom Warwick might seek to control and place on the throne. Whether Richard actually refused to be involved, or whether Warwick felt the older of the King's two remaining brothers was sufficient for his purposes, is not documented. In any case, the impression from the historical record is that Richard emerges from these years as strongly loyal to his brother Edward IV, and in 1469, aged 17, we see him campaigning with Edward's army to put down various insurrections in the North arising from this general background of tension.

It had become clear by then that Warwick, with George in tow, was behind the latest unrest. What followed was typical of the times. Temporarily outmanoeuvred, Edward IV was captured by Warwick and George, who then sought to control affairs of state. Richard, it appears, along with Edward's ally Lord Hastings, was allowed to slip away. Perhaps Warwick saw them as an irrelevance. However, Warwick's control of Edward turned out to be an illusion. Some weeks elapsed while Edward cooperated with his captors, presumably confident (or at least hoping) that they lacked the political credit to threaten him personally. In a reprise of the Duke of York's dilemma in 1460, this appears to have given time for Warwick to realise that he did not command sufficient loyalty or popular opinion in the country to sustain his position. At the same time, Hastings, Richard, and others had mobilised support for King Edward and the roles were quickly becoming reversed: Warwick and George were now in a rather awkward situation as the King's authority and freedom to act was restored to him. Fortunately for them, and for whatever reason, Edward was not vindictive: they escaped any significant reprisals at this stage. Throughout this episode, Richard appears to have been loyal and effective, and rewards followed. Within a very short time he was appointed as Constable of England. He received further grants and responsibilities, including the independent command of an army to put down insurgencies in Wales. At 17, he was becoming an important lieutenant to the King.

But 1470 was a time of severe turbulence. By March of that year, Edward was in Lincolnshire attempting to crush a local rebellion that turned out to be rather more serious than at first it had appeared. Once again Warwick and George, Duke of Clarence, were behind it. On this occasion, when the rebellions failed to take hold, these two fled to France, fearing that Edward's tolerance must surely run out. It did not stop there. By September, the kingdom was once again threatened with invasion from France, with Warwick, Clarence, and Margaret of Anjou as the principal antagonists. This time, Edward and Richard were to be surprised by the further betrayal of the Marquis of Montagu, a kinsman of Warwick. It was their turn to flee (back to Burgundy), leaving Warwick and George to enter London and reinstall Henry VI as monarch. By 1471 Edward felt strong enough to return. After an uncertain beginning, by April he had mustered sufficient troops to bring Warwick and his army to battle at Barnet. By this stage, George of Clarence had defected back to his brother, speaking volumes for the fluidity of trust and loyalty of the times – and for George personally. Outnumbered, but aided by fog, some surprise, and the luck of having his opposition attack each other in the confusion, Edward defeated Warwick, who was killed at the end of the battle. Richard's role in this had been to lead the right wing of Edward's army, and by now he was developing a reputation as a competent and reliable military leader. Whether this reputation was truly earned, as opposed to being the product of propaganda that would suit both Edward and Richard, is less clear. Some historians have argued that the solid evidence for Richard's military prowess is not as substantial as might first be assumed. That said, relatively little evidence is offered to suggest any incompetence or unreliability. At least as an individual at arms, if not as a commander, it seems he met or exceeded the expectations of the times.

The Battle of Barnet did not quell the insurrection. Margaret of Anjou was in the south-west of England, and despite Warwick's defeat and death, her party still felt confident enough to challenge Edward. Within days of the Battle of Barnet, Edward once again set out to confront another Lancastrian army. With Richard in the vanguard, Edward intercepted Margaret's army at Tewksbury in May 1471 before she could join forces with her Welsh allies. There, the Lancastrians were thoroughly defeated and, significantly, Henry VI's heir Edward was among those killed. With this victory, Edward IV had now clearly established his monarchy. Aged 18, Richard had become a significant and fully-fledged military leader in Edward IV's court. Doubtless this was due to patronage from his brother the King, but it would not have been possible without a suitable degree of competence and dependability on his part. In contrast, his brother George had proven unreliable and, unsurprisingly, was less favoured by the King.

There followed a long period where Richard's life appears more settled, although in the 1470s, that is something of a relative term. It begins with his marriage to Anne Neville. It is not clear how motivated Richard was by romance, but he was of an age to marry and this was a mechanism by which his estate and power would be increased by a wealthy wife's property. He would have known Anne from his time at Middleham Castle. In the interim she had been married to Edward, Henry VI and Margaret of Anjou's son. It seems likely that that marriage was never consummated, and in any case it had come to an abrupt end with Edward's death at Tewksbury, making her available for remarriage. If nothing else, Anne's wealth (she was heiress to a substantial portion of the Countess of Warwick's estate) would be attractive. Either way, Richard asked for, and was given, the King's permission to marry before August of that year, and then left to conduct a short military campaign against James III of Scotland.

On returning to London, he found his brother George was attempting to obstruct the marriage. It has been suggested that he even tried to hide Anne from Richard. Married to Anne's sister Isabel, George had his own plans for the Neville estate, which would have been divided on Anne's marriage. A bitter tussle followed, with little love lost on both sides. This revealed greed, ruthlessness, and little regard for the law or the people involved, and it required Edward IV's intervention to broker some form of compromise. Nevertheless, by 1472, Richard and Anne were ensconced in Middleham Castle, as they were in their childhood when it belonged to Warwick. The difference was that they now owned it as Duke and Duchess of Gloucester and Richard was preeminent in the King's council for the North.

In the years until Edward IV's death in April 1483, military campaigns in France and Scotland came and went, and his reputation as a military leader was consolidated. Predominantly, however, in his role as Warden of the Northern Marches, Richard's time was mostly taken up with supervising the King's interest in the North and consolidating his own powerbase there. He went to London only rarely. In so doing, he seems to have balanced the dangers of being absent from court (which had become an increasingly difficult environment with the decline of Edward's vigour and the nepotism of the Woodvilles) whilst maintaining his reputation as a reliable and just steward of the North. His own son Edward had been born in 1473, and there is no evidence to suggest that Richard had anything other than a stable household by the standards of the time. There is no evidence, for example, of mistresses, although this would hardly have been unusual. This does not necessarily suggest sexual repression: at least two bastard children – conceived before his marriage and thereby considered respectable by the attitudes of the day – are known. It is possible, of course, that Richard was merely discreet and the evidence has not survived. But the overriding sense, at least in his public persona, is of prudence. Specifically, there is no evidence of the hedonism for which, in comparison, Edward IV was known.

Prudence and respectability seem to be the by-word of Richard's time in the North, and he was held in esteem by the citizens of York. Certain traits emerge. Recorded incidents reflect the importance he placed upon due processes of justice and fair dealing. On one occasion, he submitted one of his own retainers to the justices of the city following a misdemeanour. On another, the City appealed to Richard to protect them from the demands of the Duke of Northumberland, in full expectation of his so doing. But we should not forget that Richard would consider it in his interests to see such incidents recorded, and possibly even exaggerated, in this way. Likewise, if we accept any sensitivity to his public image, Richard would be not be above using both direct and indirect methods to discourage less favourable records. So some degree of scepticism about such records is appropriate.

Richard's relationship with Henry Percy, the Duke of Northumberland, seems significant in hindsight because Percy was to play an important role in the Battle of Bosworth. The monarchy relied upon the power of the Dukes of Northumberland and other northern magnates such as Stanley to assist in the policing and defence of the North. However, the North had been Lancastrian in sentiment. Edward IV, with Richard as his representative, had to manage delicate diplomacy to ensure the continued loyalty of these families. At the same time, he needed to contain them in the face of their powerful instincts to demonstrate their independence and their desire to acquire yet more wealth and influence. Nor did these families worry too much about their methods and who they bullied to achieve their aims. That Richard achieved this end (even Tudor monarchs were to refer positively to the effectiveness of Richard's policy in the North), and that he did this with the often-stated admiration and loyalty of the polity at large (we shall return to magnates such as Percys and Stanleys later) points to an effective administrator and propagandist.

However, specifically in his recorded performance, this should not be read uncritically as offering evidence of Richard's earning the moral high ground, or demonstrations of Richard's principles of high-mindedness and judicial balance. First, he was known to be sensitive to how he was represented, and may have influenced the recording of his actions. Second, as his argument with Clarence over the Warwick inheritance demonstrates, he too resorted to underhand and ruthless dealing when it served his interests. The effectiveness with which he prosecuted his role in the North cannot necessarily be equated with methods that we, in the 21st century, would see as ethical. Both Richard and the people he governed would be more motivated by pragmatism and results than anything else.

One other event of this time seems worthy of note here. In contrast to Richard's consolidation of his status as a dependable brother and the King's man in the North, George of Clarence's career went sharply in the opposite direction. Already forgiven several times by Edward IV for directly treasonable acts, his capacity for duplicity and opportunism seemed undiminished. Having turned to the Lancastrians against his own family, and then swapping sides again to turn against the Lancastrians, George had even been said to have been be responsible for the death of Edward, Prince of Wales, at Tewksbury. Although this specific allegation is not substantiated by hard evidence, the sum of events suggest he was an opportunist with little or no sense of loyalty to his brothers; or anyone else, for that matter. Throughout the 1470s this brother of the king continued to entertain the possibility of allying with anyone prepared to depose Edward in his favour. Eventually, after a succession of events in which George failed to heed the warnings given to him, the King lost patience and, pressed by the Woodville faction at court, had George executed. While his brother Richard had found a modus operandi fitting for a King's brother – one apparently based upon a public display of loyalty and service – George had not. It is of course possible, as Shakespeare portrayed, that Richard was altogether more Machiavellian and skilled than this suggests, merely biding the right time to strike. This is a speculation re-examined in later sections of this book when we consider the possibility of pathological elements to Richard's personality, but at this time there is no evidence that he was seen in this way by his contemporaries.

In summary, by the time we see Richard reaching his thirtieth year, he was an important magnate in his own right and, in public at least, completely loyal to the King. Important, but arguably unexceptional. It has been said of Richard that, had he died before his brother the King, he would have merited little more than a footnote in the histories of England. He had done his duty loyally and, while he sought to extend his own power and wealth, by the standards of the times he was not unusual in what he achieved or how he went about it.

THE ADULT PERSONALITY

What of his personality? In previous chapters I argued that by the time he appeared at court, he would have developed a robust degree of self-reliance and this would be accompanied by a heightened sensitivity to threat and risk. How this developed into adulthood can now be explored a little further along four lines of argument:

RICHARD WAS AUTHORITARIAN

The accounts of Richard up to 1483 sum up to an authoritarian personality. This is hardly surprising given an aristocratic upbringing in the York household, a tutoring under the roof of the Kingmaker Warwick, and his royal status as brother to the King. But it makes it difficult to judge how extreme an authoritarian he was. Nevertheless, it does seem to have been a significant element of his personality to which contemporary accounts refer. A number of converging elements point to this. For example: his piety was considered noteworthy; he was a strong adherent of the processes of law and justice; and he proved himself later to be highly motivated (if not vindictive) in seeking strong punishments for offences. In Richard's mind, moulded as it was by an aversion to uncertainty, authoritarianism serves two purposes, some of which we will explore further in the next chapter. First, a clear adherence to the scriptures, to the law, and to the consequences of the law, all rely upon codes which had the sense of certainty. Speaking psychologically, this adherence to a cut-and-dried code leads to a much 'safer' society (that is, more secure for the adherent) than might otherwise be the case. This authoritarianism is also self-servingly consistent with Richard's search for material security. A rigid adherence to the scriptures and to the justice system serves to reinforce his status as a high aristocrat and to his unassailable right to hold great power and wealth. No surprise, then, that the rich and powerful are often authoritarian.

RICHARD ACTIVELY DEVELOPED A POWERBASE OF HIS OWN

He showed a ruthless intelligence and assertiveness in pursuing his personal interests. In her book *Richard III: A Study of Service*, Horrox paints a picture of a man who painstakingly built his security in the ownership of lands, managing the balance between largesse and *force majeur* required to hold an affinity together. The clearest example of this is the lengths he was prepared to go to extract the most advantage from his marriage to Anne Neville and the access it gave him to her inheritance. This even included dispossessing his mother-in-law and having her declared as 'legally dead'.

RICHARD WAS HIS OWN MASTER

Although it does not appear in the chronology above, we occasionally see in the historical record Richard's ability to take an independent mind. A well-documented example of this occurs in 1475, when he publicly disagreed with Edward IV's treaty with Louis XI of France. He was more than his brother's cypher. This implies an awareness of his special licence as the King's brother – especially after the death of George in 1478 – and a competence and self-confidence that goes beyond purely doing what he was told.

RICHARD WAS ASSIDUOUSLY COMPETENT

We see in Richard's performance of the role of Warden of the North a sustained period of competent, independent command. Admittedly this is strongly backed by the King's authority, but the implication of the endorsement of this role – even by Tudor historians – is that Richard knew how to conduct himself and few, if any, blemishes in his record are evident at this time. Note also, though, in his personal presentation of this professional competence, historians agree that Richard was prepared to go to some lengths to manipulate his public image.

Consequently, insofar as the scant documentation allows, Richard appears at this stage to be a competent, if authoritarian, magnate. He seems reasonably intelligent, if not particularly creative, and his ruthless assertiveness can be described as precisely what one would expect from anyone in his position. All of this is rather general, although more specific claims are being made about Richard's resilience as a function of his position as the youngest member of the family. Nevertheless, most of these descriptions could apply to almost any 15th-century aristocrat, and this book has set itself the challenge to go beyond that.

We can now explore two further areas of his psychology for a more intimate profile of Richard himself. One of these is to ask how his now-established scoliosis influenced his behaviour. This is considered in Chapter Five after a general discussion about the psychology of thought and decision-making in Chapter Four. Before that, we can ask whether Richard of Gloucester saw himself as a 'Man of Destiny'[15] and what that would mean for his behaviour and actions.

The idea that some individuals have the belief that they are destined for greatness in some form or another is not particularly surprising. We should avoid obvious figures such as Napoleon, Hitler, and Mussolini, where accounts are clouded by post-hoc reconstruction and the hubris built upon the absolute power they enjoyed. In some of these individuals there are also real questions of pathological mental states. In extremes, some people's sense of destiny lead them to believe themselves

_____

15   For man read 'person'. As it happens, most people of whom this has been said have been male.

to be a god or a messiah, but what we are discussing here is very much more common and 'normal', even if it is most usually described in people who do achieve some fame or notoriety[16]. Two interesting examples in more recent British history are Winston Churchill, who was Prime Minister in World War II, and Douglas Haig, who commanded the British forces on the Western Front in World War I. Churchill's belief in his destiny is documented as early as his schooldays at Harrow, where he openly declared he was fated to save Great Britain from disaster. Haig's diaries, and his correspondence with his mother and sister Henrietta, also clearly show he believed that God had him marked as one chosen for special things.

The mindset of believing oneself is marked for greatness is worth examination in greater detail, as is the opportunity to see its varied expression in two people so temperamentally different as Haig and Churchill. If nothing else, this serves to scope the range of possibilities as they might apply to Richard. It is easy to imagine that both Haig and Churchill would have needed in early life to develop strategies to defend their self-esteem. From his earliest letters Churchill craved love and attention from his parents (to no lasting effect); and Haig, like Richard, was the youngest and weakest of his family, and was almost certainly the object of some spiteful and bullying behaviour from his siblings. Like Richard, both had rather dominant mothers, and fathers who were, for different reasons, more remote. As a strategy to protect one's self-esteem, a belief in one's future greatness has a great deal to be said for it. Particularly when starting from a position of weakness or obscurity, the individual can see setbacks and criticisms as merely temporary; their ego is protected by the knowledge that they will one day be seen very differently. A similar psychology, projected as it is onto the audience, underlies the numerous folk stories, novels, films, and even operas where the plot is predicated upon a

---

16 This is for the obvious reason that we know much less about people who achieve little or no historical significance, and specifically whether they saw themselves as men or women of destiny.

relatively minor, but steadfast, character being ultimately revealed as royal or some such person of quality. It is a psychological defence that protects the ego from the tribulations of the present, and it can sustain an individual over an entire lifetime, many being content for recognition to wait until after their death. Consequently, this mechanism is robust and long-serving, and it perhaps would not be a surprise to find it is very much more common than we might think.

This defence mechanism protects the individual but, once in place, it also amplifies their sense of self-importance and diminishes their ability to adapt to circumstances. Events that might trigger any kind of reassessment of the individual's behaviour are more likely to be dismissed as siren voices aimed at deflecting them from their true purpose. This psychology also places any reflection and self-doubt in a similar vein: to be suppressed at all costs. Consistent with this, Haig, for example, shows very little reflexivity or self-awareness in his records and this is mirrored in the accounts of those about him. People who disagreed with Haig were likely to be castigated as devious, stupid, or dismissed with a bigoted or racist remark. Where possible, he colluded in their disappearance from the scene. On the other hand, Churchill is the more problematic to describe in these terms. He had serious moments of depression within which self-doubt most surely emerged. He was also capable of being much more self-aware in his sense of his position and importance. As for Richard, we do not know of any periods where he showed any self-doubt because the records are too thin. In the attitudes of the time, it is unlikely in any case that this would have been documented or recorded. So, on the assumption that he did see himself as a man of destiny, the comparisons of Churchill and Haig give us considerable latitude in supposing how this might have manifested itself in Richard[17].

---

17 This is an area where some historians have nevertheless allowed themselves to speculate beyond the record. For example, Paul Murray Kendall's *Richard the Third* (1955) repeatedly implies motivations and a complex mentality for which there is little reliable evidence.

It follows that people carrying a sense of destiny can become inflexible and fixed of purpose. In turn, this unshaking belief in their judgement can come across as arrogant and self-important. This is hardly surprising, since such people naturally regard themselves as superior to those around them. There is also a temptation for them to confuse blind self-interest with duty since it serves nicely to finesse any squeamishness they might otherwise experience in competing with others (often unscrupulously) for credit and preferment. In their mind, the end justifies the means. It is also a mentality that tolerates hypocrisy: persons of destiny must, by necessity, be exempt from rules that apply to 'normal' men and women when and if circumstances require, since, by definition, destiny (mystical or religious causes never being far away) is fulfilled thereby. Churchill self-documents a version of this. He recognised the extravagance of his style of living and the fact that, for the most part of his life, he was living beyond his means. But then he refused to economise by so much as a bottle of champagne at lunch (more than one actually), arguing that this expensive lifestyle was essential to a man of his exceptional abilities and status.

Another element of this mentality is that it allows individuals to function under extreme stress in the confidence that posterity will vindicate their actions. Difficult decisions can be made relatively easily. So far, so good: a sense of destiny may be an important part of strong leadership. However, unfortunately, these may include poor decisions, and in the nature of such leaders, they will be adhered to longer than they should. Although the controversy over his command is still fierce a century after World War I came to an end, Haig is a good example of this. His rigidity of method and persistence in driving attacks undoubtedly cost an enormous number of lives among his own men. His self-belief and optimism that his methods would eventually prevail – under conditions where attrition was evidently weakening his armies at least as much as it was weakening the enemy – showed little or no sign of ever being dented. Doubtless he was sustained by his sense of destiny, and in the sense that the enemy eventually sought an armistice, he eventually ended up on the winning side. But the end does not necessarily justify the means: argument raged then and now over how much he deserved praise for remaining steadfast in the face of the extreme pressures that fell upon him, and which may have forced him to sacrifice men. Yet the truth is that the war cabinet came to hold little or no confidence in his methods, and largely came to view him as obdurate and incompetent. Only luck, and a ruthlessness that saw him sacrifice any number of colleagues, some of whom deserved better, kept him from dismissal. And yet, it seems clear that he went to his grave believing he had done his duty as a man of destiny. It is equally clear that now, and at the time, that others thought a person of greater flexibility of mind and openness to new ideas might have achieved as much with far less sacrifice[18].

Churchill, in comparison, seems a more complex man. He demonstrated many of the same characteristics, but in his core he showed a greater ability to absorb and accept other points of view. And we should note that Churchill (we cannot make comparisons with Richard here because, apart from a few scribblings in a prayer book, there is little or no documentary evidence of his intellectual life) showed ample evidence of an alternative intellectual life in his writing and painting. This seems largely lacking in Haig. From a psychological point of view, Churchill seems paradoxical: the point of a 'man of destiny' mechanism is to defend oneself from criticism and uncertainty by adopting and pursuing a rigid belief system in which one's personal importance is central and in which one expects to get one's own way. This might be a better description of Churchill in the early years of the war. Certainly his energy and fixedness

---

18   In fairness to Haig, a number of commanders in this war who came to the fore being seen as innovators with more flexible intellects failed. It is not difficult to speculate alternatively that WWI commanders were dealing with what was, for the time, an intractable problem.

of purpose in the years preceding the Second World War are consistent with a man of destiny. However, perhaps by the time Churchill had already achieved great things by pulling the nation through to 1942 (no mean feat and one of great courage against the odds), he no longer felt the need for the carapace of absolutism. Since Churchill is not the subject of this book, we need not pursue this further here other than to remark that, in the comparison of Haig and Churchill, we see that any such mechanism functioning in Richard still admits to considerable variation in how it is expressed.

At the very least, we can see in this mechanism very familiar and 'ordinary' psychological processes. We do not know how strongly it appears in the population at large, or how many individuals would admit to it. However, it is a reasonable assumption that it is not uncommon in professions such as politics, where the opportunity for some definition of greatness arises, and the emphasis is upon the individual's capacity to achieve it. Taking universities as another example, many moderately successful academics (and perhaps a few less so) have sustained themselves on the basis that eventually – perhaps after their death, even – they will be revealed as leaders or creative thinkers in their field. After all, there are many such examples where precisely this has happened. In Richard's case this 'ordinary' psychology would have occurred in a powerful individual who was in a position to do something about it. He was by birthright a man of destiny in an era when people believed in destiny. From this point of view, it would have been more extraordinary and unusual if Richard had not followed his destiny (as he saw it). Not to do so would have required an effort of self-negation in a decision most of us are not called upon to make.

Therefore, whilst there is no documentary evidence to the effect, it is reasonable to assume that Richard must, to some considerable degree, have held the belief that he was a man of destiny. Indeed, how could this be otherwise? He was brought up in a politically active dynasty to believe precisely this. He may have been low in the original pecking order within the York hierarchy, but, as his own self-efficacy was proving its worth, his father and brothers were disappearing from the scene. At the very least, dogged perseverance was delivering the goods, and it could be argued for such men that surviving – being the 'last man standing' – was proof positive of the correctness of their self-belief. At the time immediately following Edward IV's death, he was the dominant individual in the realm. However, that is apart from the awkward fact that his nephew, however physically weaker and inexperienced, was actually the lawful king. My observation here, for expansion in later chapters, is that the same mechanism of predestination, with all its concentric lines of defence and its ability to render difficult decisions easy (whilst not guaranteeing the right answer), would have made it practically impossible for Richard not to try and impose himself on matters the moment he learned that his brother Edward IV had died.

Chapter Four

Richard in crisis: the psychology of judgement and decision-making

We come to the final, ultimately disastrous, years of Richard's life. These are years of usurpation, killings, rebellion, and defeat. They are also the years that define Richard as one of the most controversial of English monarchs. The truth lies somewhere between two extreme hypotheses. In the first, as Shakespeare and the Tudor propagandists would have it, Richard was always a scheming villain. From this point of view, like a poisonous snake in the bosom of the court, he hid his true nature and bided his time before striking when he had the opportunity in 1483. At the other extreme, the second hypothesis is that he was merely the 'ordinary' and loyal brother of the king who became embroiled in events after the unexpected death of Edward IV.

Using the word *ordinary* in this context is a relative term, since, as we have already observed, there is hardly anything ordinary about being the brother of a 15th-century king. The word is used here to suggest that the decisions Richard *did* make were subject to psychological processes we would recognise in the present as 'normal', even if Richard was making decisions of national significance that may involve unpleasant choices or actions. It does not help that many of Richard's motivations are not known: the lack of historical record has drawn a veil. It is unclear, for example, whether he encouraged Edward IV to execute their brother George, or whether he attempted to defend him. The point is that there would be nothing unusual in the press of 15th-century politics to mean that either course justifies a diagnosis of Richard being psychologically aberrant. But by the same token, being 'ordinary' would not necessarily make Richard a saint.

How do we decide whether Richard was normal for his times and status or whether he was some form of psychopath? Good scientific practice has it that we must have very good reason to exclude the 'ordinary' hypothesis before we can seriously consider the psychopathological alternative. As we see later, psychopathological killers are actually rather rare, even among medieval monarchs. Therefore, the question is: how would any human behave in the circumstances in which Richard found himself? Doubtless, judging in retrospect, some of the decisions he made can be seen to be questionable or plain wrong. But in and of itself, that is no evidence for psychopathology if they were judgements any person in his position could and would have made in his circumstances at the time. To help make that assessment, and in order to understand better Richard's behaviour and decision-making in the fateful years of 1483–1485 in context, the next two chapters step aside from the historical analysis to look in more detail at how our minds work. In this chapter we concentrate upon how judgements and decisions are made, and in the next, we look at the implications of that for our social interactions.

EVOLUTION AND THE GENERIC STRUCTURE OF MIND

Human evolution, in comparison to competitor species, can be seen in terms of our developing intelligence in compensation for lesser physical power or reproductive efficiency. This represents a development of two capacities in parallel. One is the ability to think, reason, and plan in a complex world to compete for resources and to protect against threat. The other is the ability to apply these skills, and skills of language and representation, to enable complex social groups to function, and for knowledge and expertise to be preserved in the culture of the society. Given that all human societies have this capacity, how is this done? A good place to start is to look at how we make judgements. It is relatively easy to demonstrate that thinking is not an abstract process. Consider the puzzle in Figure 2.

You are shown four cards, all of which have a number on one side and a letter on the other. You can only see one side of each. Which are the fewest cards you have to turn over to test the truth of the statement below?

Every card with a vowel on one side has an even number on the other.

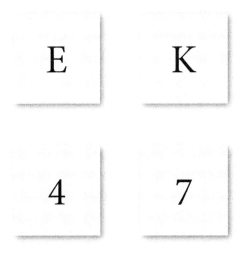

Figure 2: The Wason Selection Task.

We can see four cards where we are told there is always a number on one side and a letter on the other. We are being shown the letter side of two (E and K) and the number side of the other two (4 and 7). Now consider a further claim about the structure of the cards: *If a card has a vowel on one side, then it has an even number on the other.* What are the minimum number of cards, and which ones, that you have to turn to establish whether that claim is true? Most people correctly check what is behind the E, but a majority also turn the 4, which is logically incorrect, because a 'K' there would not invalidate the claim. Only 25% or so correctly identify the need to turn over the 7 in case there is a vowel on the other side, which *would* invalidate the claim. The originator of this task, Peter Wason[19], claimed that even attendees at a conference of Professors of Logic – people apparently trained to think in the abstract – made this mistake. However, things are different if the same problem is presented in a more familiar, concrete context, as in Figure 3.

Here, we are shown ages on one side (15 and 23) and drinks on the other (vodka or coffee) and then told that each card represents the drinks held by an individual of a given age in a bar. In this case, most people would know to turn over the cards *Age 15* and *Vodka* to establish whether the rule *Alcoholic drinks can only to be served to those over 18* is being observed. This problem is much easier, despite the fact that these two puzzles are, structurally speaking, identical.

This benefit of thinking in familiar and concrete terms goes beyond reasoning to include the ease with which we remember things. If you find remembering the colours of the rainbow hard, re-coding the sequence *Red Orange Yellow Green Blue Indigo Violet* by taking the initial letters ROYGBIV to generate the (particularly appropriate) phrase 'Richard of York Gave Battle In Vain' makes it easier. This device of re-coding from the

---

19   Peter Wason (1924–2003). A British psychologist who was in the vanguard of research into thought and reasoning in the 1960s.

You are shown four cards, each of which show a customer's age on one side and the drinks they have ordered on the other. You can only see one side of each. Which are the fewest cards you have to turn over to make sure the rule below is being followed?

Alcoholic drinks can only be served to people over the age of 18.

Figure 3: The Concrete Wason Selection Task.

abstract to the concrete is at the centre of a number of methods people use to remember things that would otherwise be difficult. Here's another: *I Value X-rays – Lucy Can't Drink Milk* is a way or remembering the sequence of Roman numbers IVXLCDM. Nonsensical, but effective.

These methods work because they use knowledge we already have to support what we have to remember. Some of this is just about making what we need to recall more likely or predictable. Suppose I gave the incomplete mnemonic 'Thirty days hath September, April, June and… ' What is next? In fact, to fit the rhyme, there are only two possible months that rhyme with September, so it is a significantly easier task than may first appear. In the case of ROYGBIV, the grammatical correctness of the phrase, combined with the interdependencies of meaning ('Richard of…', 'gave…', 'in…'), plus a repeated rhythm, all serve the same purpose. Knowledge we already have, albeit apparently arbitrary, is being superimposed upon what we have to learn to provide a structure. In these mnemonics, prior knowledge is being used to make more abstract information meaningful and thereby memorable. The prior knowledge serves the purpose of reducing what we do have to remember, while at the same time suggesting likely outcomes and experiences from memory.

This process of reducing our information processing load – by using what we already know to reduce something complex into simpler patterns – is seen in everything we do, and has been widely studied in games and puzzles. For example, in chess, where an unskilled player might see an 8 x 8 board with a bishop here and a pawn there, a skilled chess player sees familiar patterns they might describe by terms such as: *'standard King's Indian defence at move 4'*. The reference to known patterns gives every piece both a past (where it came from and how it got there) and a future (what is going to happen next in the limited range of possible ways this defence plays out). So, whereas I, as a chess novice, have to work out from scratch which of my 16 pieces I should move and what could happen in each case, our expert already knows that their choice is actually very much more limited. Moreover, for each of these moves the immediate consequences are already known because they have all been worked out and studied beforehand. This can be more than an increased efficiency purely based upon weeding out of analysis that isn't necessary. It also means the expert player can consider more factors than a novice, and altogether at a much higher strategic level in many more moves ahead. It is not so much 'what move should I do next?' but 'what kind of player is my opponent and in what style of game is he likely to be more vulnerable?' In this way, an individual who remains motivated to learn sets up a virtuous circle of learning. The more they know, the more they can learn and remember; and in turn this accelerates both the speed and capacity of learning. Experts become knowledge-rich in exactly the same way as rich tycoons become wealthier and wealthier.

This use of prior knowledge comes at a price. Again, this can be made more obvious when we contrast thinking in the real world to thinking in the abstract. Consider the following abstract logic where A, B, and C refer to undefined classes of objects. Is it *logically* correct?

> All A are B
> Some B are C
> Therefore some A are C

In the abstract, this can be hard to decide and many people will accept the above as logically coherent until it is placed in a more concrete context, as for example:

> All cars are vehicles
> Some vehicles are space rockets
> Therefore some cars are space rockets

at which point the false reasoning is obvious. If we now move on to another setting of the logical propositions:

> All men are animals
> Some animals are aggressive
> Therefore some men are aggressive

things get even more involved. The claim 'some men are aggressive' is in fact reasonable, but not as a logical conclusion from the preceding statements. In fact, many people will be unable to see the illogicality of this sequence, preferring the conclusion as proof of rationality. Our prior beliefs have taken precedence over abstract logic. Furthermore, it perhaps isn't surprising to hear that people with different experience of male aggression are likely to vary in their ability to determine the rationality of this last example, with those having stronger reasons to believe that men are aggressive showing higher likelihoods of judging the logic to be correct. To summarise, what we call 'reasoning' is not necessarily logical, and the conclusions of our reasoning are driven, at least in part, by what we already know and believe.

This issue is not trivial. In the assessment of evidence, giving a dominant role to what we already believe is the basis of bigotry and worse. This might be obvious when it comes to religious dogmatism or racism; and we might think ourselves as immune from such extremism. But it is a mistake to forget that we all reason in this way, or to think that anyone is immune to it. Examples are seen even in the most educated circles where notionally an understanding of the need for logical thinking is at a premium.

This is sometimes evident when new scientific theories are proposed in contradiction to an early orthodoxy. For example, opponents of Darwin's theory of evolution found his theory both implausible and offensive on religious grounds, resulting in insulting applications of logic. This included, famously, the Bishop of Oxford's enquiry of Huxley as to whether he claimed his inheritance from an ape through his grandmother or grandfather. Alfred Wegener, the father of modern plate tectonic theory – which argued that the shapes of Africa and South America suggested the world was a gigantic jigsaw puzzle – was largely vilified during his lifetime as the result of the refusal of the establishment to accept the logic of his claims. His theory only gained acceptance long after his death. These are specific examples, but generally we can conclude that humans often struggle to be absolutely logical and that their logic is accompanied with a fair smattering of value-laden bias. This is why, in the development of modern culture, the logic and formalism of mathematics has been seen as so important, and why society invests so much effort in teaching it to lift us above the subjectivity of everyday thought.

But we should also remember that, in the real world of survival in harsh conditions, it may be that strict logic is not as much use as experience. If evolutionary success is taken as our measure, it certainly wasn't for our ancestors, when human society was so much more fragile. Suppose, for example, an early human hears some thrashing about in the undergrowth that reminds them of the time a family member was eaten by a nasty predator. It could be a harmless (and tasty) giraffe. Do they wait to see what it is or do they run away? The payoff in this case is obvious: running may lose a few calories and it may even be embarrassing, but at least they live to tell the tale.

In practice, logicality has not been the basis on which such decisions are made because that would not resolve the untidy signals that the real world gives out. Sometimes you see the predator; sometimes you don't. Sometimes the cast of shadows in the undergrowth *looks* like a predator, sometimes it doesn't. How do we resolve this uncertainty? Rather than conducting logical analysis, it seems our minds evolved to rely upon pattern-matching: it seeks some knowledge, or past experience, that that most easily fits the welter of experiences impinging upon us in the present and then, effectively, assumes this to be the truth. This form of analysis is inside-out, rather than outside-in driven by the raw data. The outcome of this, on the basis of past experience, then serves two useful functions. Firstly, it aligns what can be a noisy, incomplete, or even contradictory array of signals into a single, coherent view. This may involve adding information that is not present (i.e. making assumptions) and it may ignore other information that is defined by that pattern as being irrelevant. Secondly, this single, coherent view gives access in memory to knowledge about how to respond if the world outside is as we think it is.

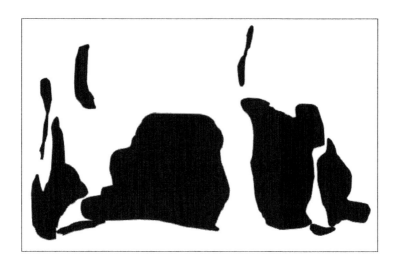

Figure 4: What is this?

This even happens in straightforward visual perception. Look, for example, at the image in Figure 4. It appears to be just a random array of black inkblots on a white background. Now turn it upside down. If you have seen this image before, you may now recognise an animal easily. It may take a while, but eventually you probably will (the answer is in this footnote[20]). What was (and remains), an abstract array of blobs is suddenly a clear perception. But the data upon which this relies has not changed and it is still incomplete! What is happening is that our perception is being driven not simply by the data itself (although clearly this has a role), but ultimately by our minds deciding what it is we are looking at. In our perception of the world, the old saying: 'I'll believe it when I see it' is better reversed as: 'I'll see it when I believe it'. You see it when you have a pattern that provides a satisfactory fit to the data. It is interesting to reflect that this process is very clear in cartoons and our experience of their realism. In fact, the images of characters such as Dumbo or Bugs Bunny are extremely unrealistic in many respects, with

20   It is a black-and-white cow.

huge areas of untextured single colours. Compared to the real world, these are extremely limited visual arrays. But sufficient information is added in key areas – for example in the alignment of key facial features or postures – to give us enough to model them as entirely coherent, complex beings.

In contrived circumstances it is possible to play with this process to understand more clearly how our perceptual system works. For example, if we strip out all of the noise in an image to make two possible perceptions equally likely, as in Figure 5, what happens is revealing in terms of what does and does not happen. Is it a candlestick or two faces? If our cognitive system was purely designed to arrive at a single solution to the question of what it is looking at, one could predict a number of outcomes. First, it might freeze, unable to identify a 'most likely hypothesis'. Alternatively, if the process was purely designed to find any solution it could, it might rest on one alone. In fact, it does neither. The system does not freeze or fail to come to a conclusion. Nor does it rest on one solution alone. Instead, revealing itself as an active, exploratory system,

Figure 5: What happens when an image represents two different things equally well.

it alternates between the two. We see this image intermittently as either the candlestick or the faces – but not both, or either simultaneously. Furthermore it is hard, if not impossible, to stop the process consciously; we cannot control the perception of seeing the image alternate between the two possibilities. In this demonstration we can see an active process searching for solutions to what it is seeing and, that being ambiguous, it keeps hunting. As we will see later, this confers some significant advantages in the real world.

Pattern-matching is an effective adaption to the problem that data in the real world is usually incomplete, variable, noisy (in the sense that any amount of interference might be present), and possibly ambiguous. Although not foolproof, the informed guesses that these patterns represent are usually correct; or at least correct enough to allow us to survive in the long run. Where there are errors, such as when we are spooked into seeing things that aren't there, these are not usually life-threatening and, as we'll see a little later, we have also evolved interesting failsafe systems to mitigate those mistakes if and when they occur. If we had not, it is doubtful we would have survived as a species.

The examples above concentrate upon visual perception and use various types of visual illusions to show how the system can be fooled. But earlier, we saw the same process applying to the way we think – one in which we do not necessarily analyse language and propositions strictly rationally, but use information within the words to suggest, and then superimpose, an understanding in the absence of such analysis. Our beliefs and past experience drive our rationality (or more correctly lack of it). This understanding will be based upon what we know and already believe. But what happens when these beliefs are contradictory? What do we do when our own thoughts are in conflict? For example, consider the following beliefs:

> That film I just saw just scared me to death
> I need a drink
> I can't drink because I have to drive home

What am I to do? Festinger[21] coined the term 'cognitive dissonance' for such conflicts in 1957, and the key issue here is how human beings deal with them to carry on functioning. They happen to all humans and we can be sure that this included Richard III. The answer is once again a question of prior knowledge and values. If our driver has recently been fined for drinking and driving, or if they hold extremely strong views on the subject of drink-driving, they may wait to calm down or may even take a taxi home. More likely is a psychological manoeuvre in which the basic problem is 'redesigned' to regain the logical or moral high ground or at least formulate a plausibly defendable[22] position:

> That film I just saw just scared me to death
> I need a drink
> I can't drink because I have to drive home
> But if I don't drink I'll be a dangerous driver in this state
> So on balance I'm doing the right thing in having a drink

This is not an argument likely to sway a magistrate to leniency, but the resolution of cognitive dissonance is a powerful psychological process which comes with commitment and belief. There are many defendants indignant that they have been punished for doing what they saw as 'the right thing'.

---

21 Leon Festinger (1919–1989). A student of Kurt Lewin's, Festinger was an American social psychologist.

22 Although subsequently many a prisoner in the dock has had the experience of discovering that skilled lawyers unpick their moral position to be neither coherent nor defendable. The legal system has developed over centuries to anticipate most of the arguments we come up with, and thereby has become clearer about where responsibility is defined to lie.

Each and every one of us shares this common characteristic of being able to adopt self-serving models of the world to process information and determine our behaviour in this way. Such examples show us how our minds will convert (and sometimes pervert) mutually contradictory propositions in order to impose a workable solution or judgement. It is interesting to note that a common theme in science fiction is to see powerful, threatening artificial intelligences self-destruct when presented with a similar conundrum. It is a testimony to human resilience that, in the same position, the human mind merely re-invents the problem and sidesteps the difficulty[23].

We have seen how human logic is distorted by what we feel and what we know. This leads naturally on to the question of how the mind deals with crisis and stress, where emotions are even more acute and more negative, as in a sense of threat. As we will see, periods of intense stress have a significant impact upon how decisions are made, and this is obviously relevant to understanding the behaviour of a person in Richard's position. He had to make momentous decisions under stress: both fateful for himself, and decisions that actually changed history. Here science is at a disadvantage. Most laboratory experiments have avoided placing participants in these situations, for the simple reason that we have strict rules of ethics that prevent us placing experimental participants in circumstances that might cause them distress. This is not to say that experiments of this kind have not been carried out. Some were carried out under the Nazi regime in utterly unethical circumstances and

23 Note that, in the last chapter, the self-belief of being a 'man of destiny' was cited as a means by which individuals continue functioning under extreme stress. The resolution of cognitive dissonance serves the same purpose. To complete that connection here, it is reasonable to say that the 'man of destiny' mentality is both a means of resolving cognitive dissonance (where long-term issues of destiny are given priority), and sometimes of *avoiding* cognitive dissonance, because that mentality keeps otherwise conflicting beliefs out of consideration.

with a dubious scientific objectivity. These must be disregarded. Others, for example those of Milgram and Zimbardo, satisfied checks on scientific objectivity and ethics of conduct at the time, but remain controversial today. The details need not detain us long. Milgram[24] was interested in the psychology of obedience, and if we take the results of his experiments at face value, his participants were prepared to administer lethal electric shocks because they perceived that someone in authority had asked them to do so. In Zimbardo's[25] prison experiments at Stanford University in the 1970s, he placed volunteer students in roles of prisoner or guard. The result was a degree of cruelty and abuse. In both of these studies, however, there must be a question as to how 'real' these situations were actually perceived to be. In any case, we are more interested here in Richard's day-to-day decision-making rather than during episodes of comparable aggression (as it happens, very few of these are actually recorded for Richard, except possibly for the execution of Hastings, covered in a later chapter). Nevertheless, real life throws up many examples of human behaviour under stress and there does seem to be some useful consensus amongst psychologists on how stress influences behaviour. Two examples follow. In the first, we see how experience can alleviate the effects of stress in quite astonishing ways, and in the second – an everyday experience most of us will recognise – we see how stress and experience are linked, and why the first example is not as strange as it first appears.

In 1998 the concert pianist Maria Joao Pires was contracted to play a Mozart piano concerto with the conductor Chailly in an Amsterdam lunchtime concert. However, as a now-famous YouTube clip demonstrates, when she sat down at the piano and the orchestra started, it was a different concerto to the one she

---

24 Stanley Milgram (1933–1984). An American social psychologist motivated by the revelations of Nazi atrocities in World War II.

25 Philip Zimbardo (1933–). An American psychologist influenced both by revelations from World War II and Milgram's experiment.

had prepared. She hadn't played *this* one for a while, and her stress is discreet (she is, after all, a professional musician on a concert platform) but evidently intense. Extraordinarily – or so it would seem – Chailly will have none of it, and somehow coaxes the pianist to sit there and get on with it. At this point she abandons herself to memory and gives a good performance. How on earth was this done? A piano concerto consists of hundreds of thousands of different notes all required to be played in the correct order and timing by two hands simultaneously. In terms of the possible combinations and sequences, the nominal memory load is absolutely enormous. That is before any considerations of musical nuance. No wonder she was stressed.

That example is deliberately misleading to make a point. The very fact that Pires was able to perform and Chailly decided to take the risk of carrying on (after all, with only a small loss of face for both of them he could easily have stopped the concert and given the pianist a copy of the score to play from), suggests that this is not as prodigious a feat as it might first seem to a non-musician. Whilst most concert pianists might be impressed by how Pires and Chailly dealt with the situation, they would also understand how it was possible. Here, the ability to manage stress, however extreme, is mitigated by the expertise that can be applied to deal with a situation. How this was done is easier explained by the second example of learning to drive.

When learning to drive, most people will be familiar with the relationship between stages of learning and stress. The common experience is that, at first, there is simply too much to process: the behaviour of other drivers; the different kinds of road layout; and control of the wheel, pedals and other instruments. As a result, most people learn to drive under dual control where they are told exactly what to do. Effectively they start by braking and steering only. Even then it is immensely stressful and often likely to go wrong. We cannot concentrate upon everything at once. Gradually, we develop habits and competencies: how to use our mirrors, how to read the road, how to change gear, and so on. Accordingly, the mental load on us gradually reduces, and with that, the stress. Our experience is that much of what we do becomes automatic (so-called 'muscle memory') and we learn to be more effective in concentrating only upon those things that really do need our attention, which in turn we are better at judging in the first place.

How is this done and what is causing the stress in the first place? One thing to note is that learning often represents a shift from active thinking and analysis to a form of automaticity. The sequence *clutch down – change from gear X to gear Y by up-across-and-down – clutch up* starts to happen without any conscious thought, in the same way as a child learns to walk or talk. If you interfere with this process of automaticity it can be disastrous – *do not* try at home thinking about which foot to put down next as you run down the stairs! In the same way, to a large extent, Pires would have been to abandon herself to a similar form of automaticity to play a piano concerto she hadn't looked at for a while *from memory*. Whilst it must have caused anxiety, it was only possible, as we shall see, because of her degree of expertise and the training she had put in previously. That is part of what professional training delivers.

This automaticity is very adaptive from an evolutionary point of view when you consider how complex the world is in comparison to our ability to process a great deal of information. In this respect humans, as the learner driver example indicates, are at first rather limited. This is one of the reasons why humans more than any other species need to protect their young for longer as they develop the necessary skills to be independent in a complex world. Translating this issue of learning to automaticity to our evolutionary ancestors, a group of hunters chasing a very dangerous animal have to process a great deal, including interpreting what the animal might do next and how your fellow hunters are behaving. If it were possible to leave some of the low-level activities – such as the ability to run through undergrowth, avoid obstacles, and handle weapons – to quasi-automatic mental processes that make fewer demands on our thinking, this would clearly be to their advantage.

We do this by exploiting two related processes. First, we learn patterns of action that do useful things without our having to think about them. There is a development of procedural skills which, with increasing practice, become both more automatic and more flexibly combined to produce more complex automatic behaviour. A trained pianist has spent hours and hours practising scales and arpeggios of all kinds in precisely the same way as a child develops motor skills such as using a spoon. Look at an infant learning to feed themself and then ask yourself when was the last time you had to think about how to do the same thing. One of the ironies of human intelligence is that we are unaware of a wide range of skills we have acquired because automaticity has made them invisible to us. By the same token, when setbacks such as a stroke take these skills away from us, if only temporarily, the effect can be devastating.

Even when actions or thoughts become automatic, learning and development does not stop producing even more complex and automated skills. In effect, continued practice has the effect of reducing sequences of procedures into a single procedure, the internal structure of which no longer enters our consciousness. For example, in the gear-shift example on the previous page (*clutch down – change from gear X to gear Y by up-across-and-down – clutch up*), a sequence of several actions becomes just one – 'drop a gear'. Psychologists refer to this as 'chunking', and although it is obviously seen in motor skills such as driving, it applies equally to any skill, be it mathematics, simultaneous translation, or even making complex decisions on the stock market.

The second skill that is being developed alongside this continued chunking and automaticity is that we learn to exploit patterns in the world to identify the fewest and most efficient chunks to process. Here is a simple demonstration you can try that demonstrates how effective this can be. Tell two friends you are going to read out a set of three-digit numbers and you want them to remember them afterwards. The numbers are 101, 112, 131, 415, 161, 718, 1920, 2122, 2324, and so on; spoken as 'one hundred and one, one hundred and twelve', and so on until the list is finished. You can make this as long as you like; the longer the better. Written down, you will more readily see what the actual structure of this sequence is, and how to extend it; and that is why this must be a spoken exercise. You then secretly tell one of the friends the information that will help them remember – the secret being that it is actually a sequence of ascending two-digit numbers starting from 10 expressed in groups of three or four, rather than two. Unless they have spotted the pattern, the uninformed friend will struggle beyond the first two or three clusters whereas the second will 'remember' everything – to the amazement of the first. So striking is the demonstration that the amazement almost always translates quickly into scepticism, the question being: 'OK, it's a trick. How was this *really* done?' But this is the power of the demonstration: the gulf between high skill and incompetence is simple: knowledge. We do not need mystical concepts such as 'a gift' or 'magic' to explain quite dramatic improvements in performance.

Actually, as you will now realise, the skilled performer is not remembering but reconstructing. The trick here is that that a complex and apparently illogical sequence can be reduced to a simple rule which means that hardly any memory is needed. And fortunately for us, a great deal of the world can be structured in such a way as to be usefully predictable, if you understand it. Understanding the world makes it easier to think about and control. This is more obvious in specific expertises such as chess or music because it is easier to compare expert and non-experts. As I remarked earlier, chess players do something similar. Rather than analysing boards by the totality of what piece is where, they see patterns describable as variations of well-worked and deeply researched positions. This allows all the locations of the pieces to be reconstructed. In this way, using legitimate games as memory tests, chess experts can easily reconstruct boards from memory compared to novices, and this is presumably a basis for the skill some of them show in blindfold playing of multiple boards. What is revealing, therefore, is that if the chess boards are *not* from legitimate play but a random layout of pieces, then the experts are no better at remembering these than novices. If they had been born with brain structures particularly able to manage chess-like puzzles, or their experience had 'grown' or 'strengthened' the parts of their brains used in chess, you might have expected that these players would still show an advantage, which they do not. I place these words in inverted commas because they are metaphors for 'done something that improves efficiency of mind' even if we do not know quite what. They are on the same level as describing thoughts as being 'on the tip of one's tongue' – it communicates what we want to say but can't be taken literally. Note that the argument here does not rely upon *disproving* the possibility that some expertise is associated with distinct brain structures. For example, recent research has claimed that taxi drivers show distinctive structures in the hypothalamus region, an area associated with the integration of spatial information. Here I am arguing how important prior knowledge is in the management of difficult, and therefore stressful, decisions. What the study of random chess boards emphasises is that while experts have knowledge, in this case it is of no value and they do not perform any better than anyone else.

To summarise, one way of looking at expertise is to see it as a trade-off between pattern-matching and analysis. Pattern-matching is mentally easy if you have the expertise (i.e. patterns) in the first place. Analysis is hard. On the other hand, when past behaviour is not entirely appropriate to the present situation, analysis is more likely to reveal it and offer a more adaptive way forward. Experts balance that trade-off better than do non-experts.

All this might seem remote from Richard III's world, and before we can start to make those links, we have to extend this theoretical digression a little further. We have considered the advantages of understanding patterns in the world – such as how a child understands how to read the emotions on a parent's face – in order to predict what is coming next and to make it easier to interpret what is otherwise an overwhelming assault of information. But what are the prices paid for that? What is the negative side of this trade-off, and specifically what role does stress play in this?

First, you can see that there is an innate conservatism in this system: humans tend to interpret the world in terms of what they already know. It is arguably the case that we can only solve problems to which we are already entertaining the correct answers (or at least the correct procedure to reveal that answer) because what we are looking to do is to match a particular solution we already have to a given problem. As I commented earlier, this can lead to fixed-mindedness and, beyond that, bigotry. For human beings, being creative and lateral thinking is not an easy thing to do, and is only possible when training to be analytical is combined with some experience that gives the individual a way of looking at the world in a different way. Arguably this is how Einstein developed his theories of relativity because he asked himself a bizarre but apposite question – what would happen if I travelled on a light beam? – and then had the technical ability to unpick the problem that emerged from that perspective.

Unfettered, this conservatism is potential dangerous. Suppose our hunters have decided they are tracking a tasty warthog through the undergrowth. They may not have seen the animal directly but have heard the grunting and rustling that warthogs make and have come to that conclusion on the basis of experience. In this way, attention is geared towards the warthog and how to kill it, and other information, such as the wind in the trees behind, is down-graded in importance. This is sometimes referred to as selective attention: the system is selecting to pay particular attention to the information it regards as most significant to what it believes is happening in the world. But threats remain – they might actually be running towards an altogether nastier animal or they may themselves be being stalked by a predator. If our pattern-matching system has fixed into one interpretation of the world, how does it protect itself from the consequences of being wrong?

As you might expect, our psychology has evolved to consider this possibility – otherwise we would surely have died out – and this turns out to have consequences for how we respond to stress. Previously, it was assumed that selective attention worked by blocking out information it regarded as irrelevant, but then researchers in the 1950s began to realise that could not be correct. For example, at a party, if someone uses your name or talks about something that interests you, you are more likely to pick that up even if you weren't consciously monitoring the conversation. Similarly, drivers often report the experience of taking avoiding action *before* actively perceiving a particular threat. This means, in effect, that our minds are, after all, monitoring material previously determined as being of no interest. It may be that this background information received only a modicum of attention, but it received some, even if we weren't aware of it. Researchers then went on to show that when such information contains something of importance to us – this may be our own name or someone shouting 'fire!' – the attentional system recalibrates to take account of the new circumstances. We selectively attend to the world according to how we *think* it is, in order to minimise the processing we actually do. This is sometimes referred to as adopting a mental model of our world. But additionally we also spend some mental resources weighing up the other options, to allow for the fact that we may have to change that model and adapt to different or dangerous circumstances.

Now when we return to stress, the conservatism of human thought and the processes of selective attention both play a part. First, any stress is intrinsically attention-grabbing, because threats or unresolved issues demand attention. Under these conditions, the mental resources available to consider alternative models of the world are reduced. Unsurprisingly, therefore, one of the first casualties of stress is a form of rigidity in which individuals are more likely to entrench in actions and attitudes which are familiar to them. Furthermore, memory is impaired in these conditions. One of the reasons why safety-critical systems have a very strong element of training and procedure is because, in a crisis, even skilled operators can forget key things or overlook important information as the stress impairs their cognitive function.

There are several good examples of this in disasters and near-disasters. At Three Mile Island, a major nuclear catastrophe nearly occurred because the controllers made the decision that a reactor was suffering from too much coolant, whereas in reality there was too little. Their perseverance in draining the coolant therefore exacerbated a relatively minor crisis, and it was a matter of good fortune that the mistake was finally detected. Part of the problem in this case was that when the reactor moved out of safe operating parameters, so many bells, sirens, flashing red indicators, and printers spewing out warning messages went off that the torrent of information threatened to overwhelm the operators.

Another good example is the crash of a BMA 737-400 onto the M1 in Leicestershire in 1989. One key aspect of this crash[26] was that, following damage to one engine, the pilots mistakenly turned off the wrong, undamaged one. Unfortunately, in these specific circumstances, many of the symptoms of the plane's distress disappeared, and the pilots did not discover the mistake until they needed power to land, by which time it was too late. For example, one of the key symptoms of the emergency (an instability caused by differential fuel supply to the engines)

---

26   In this, as in most such cases, there were a number of other factors – some beyond the control of the pilots – that converged to contribute to the crash.

disappeared when only one engine was operative. The pilots were thereby *reinforced* in the belief that they had taken the correct action and missed early opportunities to review the evidence that would have told them otherwise. To summarise these examples, stress can be the enemy of problem-solving, and in general leads to more reactionary, blinkered behaviour.

One of the things that humans find particularly difficult at the best of times is managing complex issues of degree and balance. This is for the simple reason that these problems require more processing and analysis. In a military situation, when should the commander attack and when should they wait for more advantageous conditions? When a king has information about a possible conspiracy, does he act or does he wait for the situation to unfold? Such decisions are rarely simple and usually have negative as well as positive consequences, whatever decision is made. For reasons that follow from what has already been said, it is not surprising that stress affects these decisions badly, and relatively few decision-makers manage to maintain a sense of balance. More likely, one of two things happen. In the first, the individual freezes or refuses to make any kind of decision at all, perhaps waiting to see how things unfold. In the second, the individual decides to act, and, by processes not unlike the management of cognitive dissonance, a complex problem is turned into a simple, binary one. This can lead to very destructive either-or decisions (as in *'either he goes or I go'*) rather than compromise. In the case of Richard III, one wonders whether precisely this dynamic (*'it's him or me'*) was an element behind Richard's final charge at Bosworth. But in a medieval battle for the crown, that was, in fact, true. Only one royal contender was going to survive the day.

So the effect of stress on thinking and decision-making can be very negative. Decision-makers can overlook or misinterpret key information and can make poor decisions on the basis of their prior beliefs. This regression to habitually held views or perspectives can, through the processes of cognitive dissonance, also lead to questionable logic. Chapter Six covers Richard's securing of the young Edward V at Stony Stratford and the arrest of Earl Rivers and others who were escorting him. It is quite reasonable to look at this event, and the cascade of decisions consequent upon this in an atmosphere of growing crisis, as just such an example.

One other aspect of stress is worth reporting. Recent research indicates that stressed individuals, particularly men, are sometimes prone to *increasing* their risk-taking with a corresponding increase in optimism of a successful outcome. This behaviour seems the opposite of was previously described, where stressed decision-makers stick rigidly to dogmatic and familiar solutions. But they share two key characteristics. First, it can be described as an almost culpable perseveration with a chosen course of action; and second, it often flies in the face of clear evidence that this line should be abandoned. This evidence is usually ignored. Military examples of this abound, not least in the much-repeated pattern of Haig pressing ill-prepared attacks in WWI. Politics also offers its fair share: Margaret Thatcher's resistance to abandoning monetarist policies in the first years of her premiership is arguably a good example.

Chapter Five

Richard's scoliosis: the psychology of cognition and social interaction

The previous chapter concentrated upon very general issues of cognitive function and how evolutionary pressures have shaped them. This is entirely appropriate to the line of argument that Richard could be described as psychologically 'normal' in this respect. In the next chapters we can examine how well this accounts for Richard's behaviour in the final years of his life. Before that, we must also consider how human cognition, as described, influences our social interactions. We need to do this because the proof of his scoliosis from the discovery of his burial place has important implications for Richard specifically. Bones may not respond to psychoanalysis, but it turns out in Richard's case that they may tell us something useful about the individual's psychology, and how he functioned in society.

Cognition and social interaction

Social interaction is a complex skill, as anyone watching a growing child will know as it develops from its rudimentary beginnings. Taking the previous chapter on automatised thought and behaviour, it is not surprising that its mechanisms are hard to see in operation because they are not usually available to conscious thought. We may *feel* the consequences of social interaction ('I think I irritated him'; 'I think we can be friends') but we may not always be able to describe how or why it happened, or why conversations went the way they did. Many of us are also prone to social errors of one kind or another, or simply don't know why our behaviour sometimes produces unexpected and unwanted outcomes. Many of us are socially clumsy. This is why interviewers and counsellors can be trained to be more effective in their work, and why books and articles with titles that essentially mean '*How to Manipulate the People Around You and Get On*' are so popular. This is not just about our use of language. Some might think that in humans, compared to other species, less social function is invested in public display. But fashionable clothes, facial hair, make-up, stylish dressing, and behavioural posturing are all, in some sense or another, comparable in function to the plumage of a peacock. This is an important channel of communication in social relations that we all use. They can be taken to signal[27] our social status, how we identify and place ourselves within a social framework, and even our sexual availability. Social interaction is a permanently active process in which the cognitive system is using varied channels of communication, and various cues in the behaviour of other people, to understand our social context and to guide our responses to it. Just as in reasoning, perception, and decision-making, we are using our knowledge of the world

---

27 The key point here is that signals are interpreted by, rather than imposed upon, their recipients. The process is therefore prone to error. You may have intended precisely that signal, and very often the recipient is correct at picking this up. But it also needs to be said that some signals, such as sexual availability, are easily, and sometimes wilfully, misread. In our society, responsibility for the consequences of that error lies firmly with the recipient of the signal because acting on that basis can be a serious offence, whereas the opposite miscommunication – failing to respond to an intended signal – may cause some hurt feelings but is largely harmless.

to provide a coherent model of what is going on. In a dynamic social system, we need to know the intentions and wishes of the people around us. Most of this is taking place in real time, and for the same reasons that apply to human thought and judgement, we will see that it is subject to systematic biases and errors. Understanding these processes is important because there is good reason to speculate in Richard's case that his scoliosis added a specific dimension to these biases and errors and had specific consequences for the quality of his social interactions.

Returning to the general business of social interaction, one of the most fascinating things that the study of psychology reveals is just how much expertise and information processing is being applied on a second-to-second basis without our really being aware of it. For example, in the 'cocktail party effect'[28], which relates to the process of selective attention, it is surprising to realise how sensitive we are to specific speech within the background hub-bub of a social gathering. If someone mentions your name, or something of direct interest to you, then the likelihood is that you will notice it and pay attention to what they are saying. And yet, otherwise, if you were asked later what people nearby were talking about, you are likely to say that you don't have the faintest idea because you weren't paying attention to it.

How is that done? How can it be possible that we ignore background conversations, yet at the same time, we are instantly aware when they become relevant to us personally? The answer is counterintuitive: it cannot be that we simply shut irrelevant conversations out, because in that case we would never be able to notice when they become relevant. In fact, our mind is doing a great deal of monitoring of so-called 'ignored' material. Speaking in terms of evolutionary benefit, this makes perfect sense. If we did not do this when attending to something, we

---

28   This dated label reflects the late 1950s and early 1960s when this area was first a focus of psychological research and when cocktail parties would be a familiar social event. Today, researchers can't afford cocktail parties, and probably wouldn't go anyway.

would be extremely vulnerable to (as yet) unnoticed threats. It is all very well to concentrate upon the warthog you would like for lunch as you chase it through the undergrowth, but if you fail to notice the grizzly bear that is chasing you, the question of what or who is for lunch is moot. So it turns out that, although we are not easily aware of it, something in our mind is constantly monitoring all sorts of background information to make sure that we understand what is going on, or that some rapid reappraisal isn't in order.

This applies to social environments as much as anything else. The constant need to consider the possibility of reappraisal applies strongly to interpersonal communication. This is partly because communication and cooperation between individuals takes place in real time. As a result, noise and other interruptions mean that not all messages are received reliably. All the time, we have to work out, and check, that we know what is happening. Again, the interest lies in how practised and adaptive humans are in this respect. These skills work both for maximum fluidity and also as a natural correcting mechanism. Precisely because it is so effective, the fluidity of this mechanism is hard to see. But if, for example, you watch two workmen lifting and placing heavy objects, a serious of grunts, monosyllables, and gestures get the job done when no clear instructions have been articulated. And in case you thought this was just the province of physical labour, precisely the same communication devices are used by a conductor rehearsing a symphony orchestra. Good conductors are valued for their efficiency and the time they save in rehearsal by communicating what they want non-verbally in real time. In both cases, it is also worth reflecting that, had it been necessary for that communication to be conducted by a series of accurate and unambiguous statements, it may not even have been possible – verbal exactitude and getting things done do not always go together.

Such a fluid system allows for the possibility of error. Some of the most hilarious anecdotes between orchestral musicians involve players misreading the conductor's intentions. Sometimes an extravagant chopping motion does not mean 'clash the cymbals as hard as possible' but the reverse. Thankfully, most people beyond childhood do not make many mistakes in social interactions serious enough to require correction and further training. But they can be revealing when they do occur. A personal example: some time ago, at a parent-teacher meeting, a maths teacher opened with the statement that 'Your son is revolting'. Within milliseconds, he had clearly realised that he was being misunderstood. Something in my body language was not what he expected and he was quickly able to work out what had gone wrong. He went on to explain that this was, in fact, a good thing. The school had made a mistake over curriculum and, my son was making a fuss about being in PE lessons when he should have been in maths. The anecdote reveals a great deal: the error originates from the maths teacher assuming I knew what he was talking about; my response (whatever it was) was based upon a different understanding of what the teacher meant; and the instantaneous correction reflects that teacher's ability to read the signals implicit in my reaction to work out what the misunderstanding was. Human beings communicating with each other make assumptions about what the other intends by what they say and do, and use the signals they receive back to monitor the extent to which their intentions are being understood. Mutterings such as 'ah-hah', 'of course', or 'I see' generally offer confirmatory support, whereas 'hold on', 'mmmmm', or facial expressions of sheer annoyance are generally taken in the opposite way.

All of this is consistent with the broader view of human cognition: the message here is that the interpretation of social cues, speech, and body language is not neutral. Rather than waiting for information and then hoping to work out what it means, we are proactive. On the basis of minimal cues we make assumptions and then work on the basis that they are correct until proven otherwise. In the parlance, we are *modelling* our world. The huge evolutionary benefit of this is that it resolves problems of inconsistency, as we found in the previous chapter, as well as giving a general frame of reference to the interpretation of incoming information.

Social cues are therefore important in communication, and sometimes individual idiosyncrasies in the cues people put out can have a significant bearing on the perception of their personality in general. More than one romantic lead actor in silent movies failed to make the transition to talkies because their weak and reedy voice undermined their image. Sometime, the effect is even more specific. Amongst television and radio interviewers, Margaret Thatcher was seen as a hard case. Even the very best among them felt that, too often, they came out second best in interviews. It appears that the root of this lay in Thatcher's use of auditory cues in conversation.

Psychologists are often interested in the concept of 'cues' such as hesitation, changes of pitch, or emphasis, in speech. These might indicate how far the individual is from a natural closure in what they are saying, or they may indicate that they are about to hand over their 'turn' of speaking to their interviewer. In this case, researchers observed that Thatcher had, in fact, radically overhauled her manner of speaking. In her early career, her voice was generally perceived as rather shrill and off-putting. Consequently, before she became Prime Minister, she undertook a course of voice training in which the fundamental frequency of her voice was lowered significantly and her speech was also slowed down. This had consequences. One of these was to disrupt the reliability with which the cues she used in speech could be interpreted. For example, she would typically throw in an emphasis or false closure which was taken as indicating, incorrectly, that she was about to finish her turn of speaking. The result was that the interviewer, misreading her actual intention, would interrupt. This would be followed by an admonishment that she had not finished. One-nil to Margaret Thatcher! Arguably, an element of her reputation as a powerful, if hectoring, presence in the media is the unforeseen consequence of elocution lessons.

We do not, of course, know what Richard III sounded like in conversation, but we can speculate about how his scoliosis will have impacted upon his interactions. The condition, as revealed by the curved spine of his skeleton, was quite severe and probably emerged in adolescence. It is unclear whether this caused him pain: apparently sufferers of this degree of scoliosis are more likely to experience muscular back pain, but it is not always the case. At the time of writing, a prominent example of someone unaffected by their scoliosis is the World Champion sprinter Usain Bolt, and it has been suggested that general fitness and development of core muscles may mitigate the effects of the scoliosis. The configuration of the pelvis and leg bones in Richard's skeleton indicated that there was unlikely to be a limp, and his shoulders would be only slightly asymmetrical. This could probably have been concealed once tailors and armourers had adjusted his clothing with padding. It is therefore noteworthy that few contemporary references are made to any asymmetry, although there are some[29].

In any case, we might be less interested in the *degree* of Richard's affliction than the fact of any physical deformity at all. In the 21st century, the term 'deformity' is not considered politically correct because, as in the case of skin colour, ethnicity, and gender, making negative attributions on the basis of superficial aspects of appearance is seen as unfair and unacceptable. Not so in the 15th century. Then, it was generally believed that any departure from a 'normal' appearance was seen as a reflection of the condition of one's inner being or soul. To identify someone as deformed was to make a moral judgement about their personality being weak, insufficiently formed, or, in the worst cases, twisted and evil.

---

29 Rous, a contemporary (although not unbiased) commentator, comments that his right shoulder was higher than his left. It is also noteworthy that 'crookback' is added to Sir Thomas More's description of Richard 20 years after his death. It seems unlikely that this was complete fabrication. More likely he was merely reflecting (albeit possibly amplifying) a perception already in common memory.

Some of this prejudice lies historically in a strongly hierarchical view of human society that persists to the present day in various forms of prejudice. As recently as the 20th century, a significant number of British people still believed, for example, that women were less capable than men in making political judgements and therefore should not have the vote. Distinctions were also drawn within gender. Numerous writings in wartime, be it in Wellington's army or during the Great War 100 years later, refer to the distinction between officers and men. Ideal officers were 'gentlemen' and words such as 'gallant' or 'noble' might be used to describe them, when 'scum' and 'rabble' might be used for the private soldier. At best, the terms 'brave' or 'disciplined' might be applied to these men. The distinctions were also visible physically: on average the officers in the Great War were several inches taller than the men they led, for example. Today we can interpret this in terms of a superior diet and living conditions in childhood, but at the time it only served to emphasise the accepted differences between the 'officer class' and men. In 15th-century England, such divisions were deeply embedded in society and the aristocracy were effectively a different caste, which, as I argued earlier, is not without some genetic justification. It is undoubtedly the case that such attitudes and beliefs, despite the intervening developments in genetics and sociology, persisted into the 20th century and are held by some today.

However self-serving the argument may have been, the medieval aristocracy genuinely believed that to be born into a noble family was to be a superior human being, and that any physical weaknesses they observed in the lower classes was an expression of their lower status. Such a belief goes hand in hand with a propensity for authoritarianism and high-handedness, which, if not entirely eradicated, is far less acceptable in the 21st century than it was in the 15th. This makes it difficult to interpret the behaviour of historical figures in context because the values that went with it were so ingrained in society. For example, in the 17th century, the new generations of scientists would regularly dissect live animals such as dogs as part of their investigations. They believed that the dogs, being so low in the biological pecking order, had no soul and therefore no consciousness. They explained the desperate distress shown by the animals as no more than a simulation of human distress[30], and sought to ignore it.

For all of its advantages, rank comes with obligation and expectations. What makes Richard's scoliosis notable is that he was a significant aristocrat. What would be seen in a peasant as run-of-the-mill degeneracy common to his status, requires explanation in a prince. He will naturally have power and ambitions that matter, and conditions such as scoliosis were taken to mean something. It was not possible – easier in modern times – to put the condition down to the luck of the genetic draw, because the scientific understanding of the time did not permit it. The universe of the 15th century was not run by chance. Therefore, either the deformity was the devil's work and bodily deformity was the mark of a twisted and evil soul, or it expressed God's mysterious ways. As an act of God, this does not necessarily imply a personal punishment. In the 15th-century mind, the turmoil of a civil war in which anointed kings were deposed represented a perversion of God's order. A degree of indiscriminate suffering might equally be an expression of God's judgement on society. Thus the death of individuals such as Henry VI and Edward V – in the latter case, a clearly innocent boy – were seen as the price of sins committed by their ancestors. In this respect, there was no shortage of sins, and memories were long. In the late 15th century, such references could easily go back to the deposition of Richard II in 1399. At that time, everything had a reason, even if it was a mystery known only by God.

What do devout, well-educated Christians such as Richard of Gloucester think when their scoliosis becomes apparent? It

---

30   Another element of the belief structure was that all lower creatures sought to raise themselves in the hierarchy. Thus fossils were interpreted as rocks simulating creatures, and animals such as dogs or apes emulated humans.

seems unlikely they would consider themselves fundamentally evil and thereby self-consign their immortal soul to hell. Modern criminologists refer to a concept of 'labelling' in which individuals come to see themselves as criminal or evil because they have been repeatedly defined as such by the authorities, which merely increases the likelihood of criminal behaviour in these cases. The tendency to see the self-as-evil, as opposed to the self-as-pious, represents a 21st-century emphasis on the self as a free agent to choose criminality. In contrast, Richard's upbringing as a prince and leader of men – for whom the duty to God and the law was paramount – would lead to a simple model of piety with no conception of alternatives because the loss of one's immortal soul was unthinkable. This would be only the more so if Richard saw himself as a man of destiny. From Richard's point of view, resolution of cognitive dissonance is far more likely to lead him to an acceptance that, even if God's exact purpose was obscure, he must fulfil his duty as a leading member of a royal family. Wherever that duty leads, the ends would justify the means.

With respect to Richard's scoliosis, the problem beyond his self-perception was that he would also have been aware that it was not only *his* problem. One of the more powerful biases in social psychology is the so-called attribution bias. Suppose you are driving along a road and a car behind you begins to flash their lights and impatiently overtake you. For most people, the most likely response is to come to the conclusion the driver is an aggressive, antisocial idiot. Would they consider the possibility that he or she had just received a call from hospital where their daughter is in intensive care? Unlikely. The *fundamental attribution error* being committed here is a general tendency for us to attribute other people's behaviour to basic dispositions of personality such as greed or selfishness rather than consider causes based upon external circumstances.

The simplest way to understand such biases falls in line with previous accounts of human psychology: it is a cost-effective way of using our powers of cognition. It is generally easier to attribute traits such as greed or aggression than it is to analyse their behaviour in terms of specific situational factors. Pattern-matching ('he is behaving like an aggressive driver') is much easier than trying to work out what could be happening to lead a perfectly reasonable person to behave so erratically and without consideration for others. Furthermore, not only is that processing harder – it is much more likely to be incorrect. Our experience is simply that there are a lot more drivers on the road who are selfish and aggressive than there are those desperately trying to get to hospital. The easiest conclusion to draw is also the easiest to understand and live with, and the most probable. Sadly, and particularly in the case of driving, where the opportunities for receiving further information that explains what is actually going on are so few, the outcome is to amplify aggression.

Returning to Richard, it is not difficult to see that, given that his scoliosis was visible to some at least, he would be presented with specific social disadvantages. There would be an increased likelihood for those meeting him to attribute negative characteristics to him such as deviousness or evil intent. This is in the context of an already awkward social position: any dealings with a person of Richard's status, even before his elevation to monarchy, would be influenced by the implicit threat encompassed by their status. Just being in their society was a risk, let alone the consequences of actually offending them. Consider, for example, the quasi-judicial murder of Ankarette Twynyho and John Thuresby by George of Clarence on a trumped-up charge of poisoning following the death of his wife. They were probably entirely innocent victims in Clarence's broader claims for power. Indeed, it has been said that some aristocrats deliberately preferred staying away from royal courts up to, and even beyond, Elizabeth I's day because they were such a dangerous places to be, despite the potential benefits of attendance on the monarch.

Such situational threats can induce debilitating caution. As a simple experiment, ask yourself what your response would be if you were asked to do a simple act such as typing your address on a keyboard, but that the smallest error would be punished by an immediate electric shock. The answer would be that you would be extraordinarily careful. Typing would be exceedingly slow and probably with one finger. Paradoxically, it is even possible that the likelihood of error is *increased* in such circumstances. The issue is not dissimilar to those of unwanted obtrusive thoughts. For example, many people (usually more represented on the neurotic scale) have a real fear that, while they are not suicidal, they will throw themselves under the train as it enters a platform. Nor are we far away from the concept of a 'Freudian slip' or parapraxis, in which a preoccupying and socially unacceptable thought is inadvertently expressed. A classic might be to name an ex-wife in a second marriage ceremony. In these cases, the fear of mistake captures the individual's attention, leaving less mental capacity for other things, including self-censorship. When the risks are very high, a trade-off between fluidity and accuracy leads to very controlled and cautious behaviour with a greater chance of bizarre outcomes.

The logic follows that personal dealings with King Richard III, even ignoring his scoliosis, would never be easy. Even before his summary execution of Hastings, or his vindictive prosecution of Rivers and the others, he was clearly of his type: powerful, status-conscious, and with a capacity for ruthlessness. It is possible his closest confidants (who were relatively few by the time of Richard's monarchy) were able to be reasonably comfortable in his company. However, where there was a lesser degree of familiarity, Richard's social interactions were always going to be stilted. What makes this more of an issue is that, particularly in his last three years of life, any such inhibition is part of a more toxic mixture. As time goes on, many of his close advisors, most of his family, Hastings, Buckingham, and others, are gone or alienated by rebellion. A continued reliance on his northern associates and the increasing discontent of those in the south adds to this. Any reputation as being vindictive and murderous is being fed by the knowledge of what happened to Hastings, Rivers, and the rest, including speculation as to the fate of Edward IV's sons. This can only have had a negative impact. Any interaction in this context will be difficult.

On top of this, any notion of Richard's deformity – however slight – is merely feeding into an existing tendency for people to attribute to him a malign and devious personality. Part of the toxicity here is that the combination of the discomfort any individual would experience speaking to a powerful man of such a reputation, coupled with the knowledge of his deformity, will exaggerate the negative effects of both. In what is called *confirmation bias*, and entirely consistent with the pattern already described, the cognitive system seeks confirmation of currently held beliefs. Thus, Richard's reputation, deeds, and deformity can all be taken to reinforce a belief of malignity. Such psychological drivers can only be divisive, and their effects are felt on both sides of a social exchange. Richard, who in all probability was aware of what influence these factors would be having, would perceive both a defensiveness and caution in people he dealt with. But he is unlikely to be immune to attribution biases himself, and as a result is more likely to develop a sense that the other person is devious and not well-intentioned. Being naturally vindictive and probably subject to a degree of paranoia as his troubles multiply, the outcome can only be of increasing alienation on both sides.

I may be overstating the impact of Richard's scoliosis, but the point is that we can be sure that, however slight the effect, it will not have helped Richard's need to form strong and trustworthy associations upon which a longer reign would have relied. It seems reasonable to suppose that in the context of his Wardenship in the North, which was longer and for the most part uncontentious, any such problems were nullified by familiarity over time coupled with the success of his formal role.

Bear in mind also that when he started that role, his scoliosis may not have been detectable, even to himself, given his age and the likely date of its onset. When, from 1483 onwards, he was reliant on a less familiar social environment and his actions were far more contentious, his scoliosis is much more likely to have been a material factor, to the extent that we can see at least one reason for any behavioural discontinuity between Richard prior to 1483, and Richard as Protector and King.

Chapter Six

The unravelling: the events of 1483–1485

The death of Edward IV on April 9ᵗʰ 1483 marks a clear separation between the first thirty years of Richard's life and the final two that have defined the reputation of King Richard III. In this chapter we concentrate upon the historical events, which are complicated enough in themselves. The next chapter then looks at Richard's state of mind as these events unfolded. For reference and clarity, a summarised timeline for 1483 is provided at the end of this chapter.

Edward IV died aged 41, leaving his 12-year-old son Edward as his successor. His final illness seems to have taken people by surprise, and, given existing tensions at court and the age of the new King, a dangerous political vacuum emerged. Forseeing the risks to his dynasty, Edward IV is said to have made efforts in his last days to reconcile the factions of the Woodville family on one side, and the established aristocracy (led by his old friend Hastings) on the other. For the same reasons, he was commonly believed to have left his inheritance and the well-being of his heir in the protection of his remaining brother, Richard of Gloucester, although documentary evidence of this has not survived.

With news of the King's death arriving at Middleham in mid-April, the relative stability of Richard's life in the North came to an abrupt end as events unfolded rapidly. Any messages coming from influential members of court, such as Hastings, would have spoken urgently of getting to London as quickly as possible, preferably with Edward V in tow. His correspondents would expect a sympathetic and proactive response to their cause: with no reassuring news from the dead King's council, Richard would be concerned that the Queen and the Woodville faction would effectively pursue a coup d'etat by seeking to crown the new King and control him in his minority. Given the Woodville family's record in the latter years of Edward IV's reign, this was entirely in character and would represent a direct threat to Richard and his family, as well to many other noble families. To have stood by quietly at this stage would have been to cede actual and moral authority to the Woodvilles, and that could have cost Richard his power, possessions, and even his life. He would also see it as an affront to his role as Protector. After all, given that Edward IV was dead and Edward V was just a boy, Richard was de facto the most powerful man in the state.

Looking beyond a threat to his person, there was also every chance that Edward's death would once again lead to a civil war. The established nobility resented the Woodvilles as avaricious upstarts and felt threatened – as well they might – for much the same reasons as Richard himself. It would be natural for them to seek support and alliance with Richard, who had the additional advantage of legally representing the status quo and the stated justice of the last King. In practice, Richard was placed publicly in opposition to the Woodvilles by default. Consequently, very soon after Edward IV's death, Richard apparently received news from Henry Stafford, Earl of Buckingham, that he would support him, with men if need be. Possibly there were others. Edward IV may have brought order and control to a country destroyed by civil war. However, in subsequently failing to control his wife's family, or to reconcile them to the established nobility, his legacy was yet another internecine struggle.

By about April 20th, Richard had assembled an entourage and started to move southwards to London. His aim, at least for public appearances, would be to assert his role as Protector. Presumably he would have been in communication with allies to coordinate their actions as he moved south. At the same time, Earl Rivers, the Queen's elder brother, was accompanying Edward V from Ludlow to London with the likely aim of crowning him, pre-empting Richard before he had time to establish his authority as Protector. However, with both parties behaving legitimately at this stage – at least in public – neither party stood to gain by acting as if the other was operating in bad faith, whatever the truth of the matter. As a result the two journeys were coordinated, which in hindsight seems strange, given what was to follow. While Richard was in Nottingham, some communication took place between him and Rivers, with the clear understanding that they would meet in Northampton. What each hoped or expected would happen from then on is unclear. Of the two, Richard had the clearer role to play in the short term in following his dead brother's instructions in the role of Protector; although he would have been aware of the hazards of Protectorship from fairly recent history[31]. Rivers, on the other hand, knew that his position was even more delicate: his family attracted no strong loyalty in either the nobility or the merchant class, and should their strategy fail, they would be in an extremely difficult position if their behaviour was regarded as treasonous. By Edward IV's edict, that could include anything that appeared hostile to Richard.

What actually happened was that Rivers, even though he was commanding the larger force and holding the young King Edward V safely away from Northampton, lost the initiative. Arriving at Northampton, Richard discovered that Rivers and the King were in fact in Stony Stratford, nearly a day's march closer

31   Neither in 1377 when Richard II was 10, nor in 1422, when Henry VI was an infant, did a Protector enjoy the uncomplicated control of the levers of state.

to London. As the new King's envoy, Rivers duly turned up with a small party to apologise for the King's absence. He explained that Northampton was not big enough to accommodate both the King's and the Protector's retinue. Whether Richard accepted this explanation or saw it as a thin excuse for Rivers stealing a march on him is a matter of conjecture. Nevertheless, by all accounts a reasonably sociable evening followed before Rivers took to his bed.

He woke to find himself under house arrest with no way of sending word to his party in Stony Stratford. Richard and Buckingham had already ridden there to intercept Edward V before he left for London. They made the appropriate fealties and, despite the ranks of Woodville force, announced that they were taking custody of him. Richard may well have reminded Edward that he was the rightful Protector by his dead father's edict. The senior Woodville nobles, Lord Richard Grey and Sir Thomas Vaughan, allowed themselves to be arrested and taken to Northampton. Despite being the larger force, Rivers' army stood aside and now apparently drifted away. Such are the facts. How Richard and Buckingham actually pulled off this coup is not recorded in detail and can only be a matter of speculation. Perhaps Rivers and the others knew all along that their political position in the country was too weak and that, despite their temporary advantage, no good would come of defying Richard in his formal role.

Subsequently, perhaps awaiting news that it was safe to enter the capital, Richard delayed arriving in London until May 4th. By this time some of the remaining Woodvilles, on the news of Richard's coup and the threat it represented to them, had fled abroad. The Dowager Queen and Thomas Grey, Marquess of Dorset, made for sanctuary at Westminster after first plundering the Treasury for the late King's considerable wealth. So much for their good faith and any good faith they presumed in Richard. It is not difficult to deduce from this that relations between Richard and the Woodvilles had been poor prior to Edward IV's death.

Richard's priority for the following weeks was to establish his authority in London as Protector, working to stabilise government when factions were seeking to exploit the vacuum left by Edward IV's unexpected death. Edward V was sent for safe-keeping to the Tower of London, which at that time was a suitable place for the purpose, and his coronation was quietly postponed. Since we are concerned here with an accurate chronology of the weeks preceding Richard's accession to the throne, we can leave for now the question of an ulterior motive for this act.

Any calm in this interregnum did not last long. One way of describing the 15th century is that it is marked by individuals in the nobility who regularly challenged each other – and the monarchy – in the pursuit of power and wealth. Unsurprisingly, therefore, and given the instability generated by Edward IV's death, fault lines and disunity in Richard's Council seem to have appeared by the beginning of June. Some of these were to be expected – Richard had brought in outsiders, close associates of his own, to work alongside established council members. Arguably he was an outsider himself. Many of the Council had worked closely with the previous regime and particularly with the Queen, who was now in Sanctuary. Resentment, pride, and a sense of entitlement was to be expected from those whose fortunes seemed to be in decline or in the balance. After the events at Northampton, where he played a central part, the Duke of Buckingham's rise to the centre of power may also have unsettled individuals as Richard showed particular favour in his direction[32]. What we do know is that, reflecting the rising sense

---

32 In this, insofar as Buckingham eventually rebelled against him, Richard's judgement was ultimately to be proven poor. Perhaps at this stage Richard could not afford to be too fussy about who offered him support, and may always have been aware of Buckingham's limitations. It is worth noting that Edward IV had conspicuously avoided giving this powerful noble responsibilities at court, and had, arguably, insulted him by forcing upon him a Woodville bride.

of uncertainty, tension, and threat at this time, Richard wrote to allies in the north to send an army to come to London as quickly as possible.

Whatever the background, what followed was shocking at the time and is central to any analysis of Richard's nature. At a meeting on Friday June 13th, Richard announced that a Woodville-led conspiracy had come to his attention. He directly accused Hastings, Stanley, the Bishop of Ely, and the Archbishop of Canterbury of treason. All bar one – Hastings – were taken away for immediate imprisonment. Hastings was warned of his immediate execution, quickly given the services of a priest, and then beheaded outside. It was a legal act by the standards of the time and accepted as such, but it was disturbing both because of its brutality and the fact that Hastings was previously Richard's friend and ally. Before that, Hastings had been one of Edward IV's most valued confederates. In fact, according to Edward IV's wishes, he was subsequently buried close by him.

One hypothesis is that Richard was pre-emptorily striking to remove an obstacle to his own ambitions. Another (not mutually exclusive) is that he was reacting to a conspiracy amongst his closest allies. Recent research[33] suggests a plausible basis for such a conspiracy that would have led Hastings into an alliance with Richard's enemies. This line of reasoning hinges on news given to Richard some days before Hastings' execution by Richard Stillington, Bishop of Bath and Wells. He is said to have told Richard that Edward IV's marriage to Elizabeth Woodville was void because of a previous marriage. In that case, it followed that Edward V and his brother Richard were illegitimate, and that he, Richard, Duke of Gloucester, was rightful heir to the throne. In one scenario, Hastings had this intelligence sometime earlier, and is being accused of attempting to keep this news from Richard. That would be treasonous in itself, but the implication

---

33 *Richard III and the Murder in the Tower* P. Hancock (2011) The History Press UK, ISBN 978-0-7524-5797-0.

was further that Hastings sought to keep Richard in ignorance in order to gain power through control of a young King whom he knew to be illegitimate. In that case, Richard would see three treasonable crimes – one against his person, one against the state, and the third against God.

Whatever the truth of any conspiracy, subsequent relations between Richard and Queen Elizabeth were hardly improved, and it required a show of force at Westminster Abbey, threatening a violation of sanctuary, to compel her finally to give up Edward V's brother Richard on June 16th. He was then transferred to the Tower with his brother. By this time, Richard also felt strong enough to see through the decision to execute Rivers, Vaughan and Grey, whom he had arrested at Stony Stratford in May.

Richard was acting fast. It has been said that a headcount of four was a small price to pay for the stability of the realm in the 15th century. Certainly many more may have died if civil war had broken out at this stage. And, by way of comparison, we may also point to the numerous executions that followed Henry VII's accession. This makes the point that, compared to other contested transitions, there is nothing here to suggest that Richard was unusually ruthless for a medieval monarch. True, there is a grim momentum to Richard's actions at this stage, but the question is whether anyone else in his position would, or could, have behaved more effectively. He occupied centre stage in London by dint of his role as Protector, appointed by the late King and now ratified by the Council. Whether or not Richard believed in the bastardy of Edward V, what was he to do next? When his father, in a similar position, claimed the crown, his supporters did not approve and he had to back down. That could occur again. Claiming the throne risked accusations of usurpation. But the alternative was also problematic. Allowing Edward V's coronation to proceed would be to cede power to a minor – one possibly tainted by illegitimacy. With strong links to the Woodville family, Edward might also be difficult for Richard to control in his role as Protector. Finally, Edward would shortly reach an age of majority, at which point Richard's position would, at best, be uncertain as the power of the Woodville family asserted itself. Becoming Regent would almost certainly lead to trouble before too long.

By June 22nd, Richard's course of action seems to have become clear. On that day, Friar Ralph Shaw, a man of influence in London, gave a sermon at St Paul's Cross, a location where speeches of consequence were not uncommon. It could not have been given without Richard's approval. In it, Shaw declared Edward V to be the bastard son of an illegitimate marriage and thereby established Richard (George of Clarence's progeny being excluded by attainder) as the true heir to the throne. On the following two days, Buckingham addressed first an assembly of the Lords and then the influential citizens of London to the same effect. This allowed Richard and his advisors to gauge that public opinion was moving to the consensus that Richard's accession was acceptable (or at least tolerable as the best course of action). Had that not been so, as happened with Richard's father two decades earlier, Richard and his advisers would presumably have acted more cautiously. Whether the general public actually believed Shaw's sermon or, more likely, accepted it for a political manoeuvre, is hard to judge. In the short term, it was unlikely to matter: Richard had cowed his opposition. On June 25th, also at the instigation of Buckingham, and presumably with Richard's approval, an informal gathering of Parliament unanimously agreed to petition Richard to assume the throne. On Thursday of that week, June 26th, this petition was read to Richard at Baynard's Castle, and, with an appropriate show of humility, he consented to accede as King Richard the Third. With his Queen, Anne, he was formally crowned on July 6th at Westminster Abbey. His reign was destined to last a little over two years.

Almost immediately, Richard began to progress around the country, taking in Oxford, Gloucester, Tewksbury, Worcester, Warwick, Coventry, Leicester, and Nottingham, before moving north to spend considerably longer in York. By October he was moving south to Lincoln when news was brought to him that none other than the Duke of Buckingham (amongst others) was rising in revolt against him. Buckingham's aim in this is unclear. He may have had pretensions to the throne himself. He may have seen enough of Richard to come to the conclusion that he had backed the wrong person. Whatever his reasons, at some stage he seems to have agreed to support Henry Tudor's claim to the throne. It is possible that John Morton, Bishop of Ely – a schemer already implicated in earlier plots – was involved: by accident or design, Buckingham had become Morton's jailer following the conspiracy that lead to Hastings' death. It seems possible that his influence now drew Buckingham into a plan in which revolt would be raised across the southern counties, the south-west, and from Buckingham's Welsh base.

As it happened, Buckingham had neither luck nor popular support. Advancing a short distance, his already unenthusiastic army was immediately harassed by forces loyal to the crown. Poor weather and guerrilla fighting seem quickly to have sapped their morale. Within days the army had melted away and Morton had fled abroad, giving Buckingham's cause up for lost. Buckingham himself was eventually captured as a fugitive in Shropshire, having been betrayed by a reward-seeking servant. He was promptly tried and executed in Salisbury on November 2nd despite his pleas for mercy and for an audience with Richard. He got neither. Other simultaneous uprisings, albeit not well-coordinated with each other, were quickly suppressed and Richard was back in London by the end of November in firm control. Following Edward IV's example, Richard's response to the rebellion was not particularly punitive. A few leaders were executed, but many, including Morton himself, were offered clemency and even some restoration of their estates[34].

---

34 This seems something of an anomaly, since Richard often showed a vindictive tendency in similar circumstances. It may be that he needed to gain the loyalty of some of the individuals he spared as he sought to establish his rule.

Insofar as any part of Richard's short reign was quiet, this rebellion was followed by a relatively quiet period. That said, from this time onward, Richard was aware of the need to prepare for an expected invasion by Henry Tudor, and the allegiance of any number of significant figures was open to question. The time is marked by a great deal of travelling and a busy legislative programme. Throughout this, the major noble families did rather well out of Richard, receiving large donations of lands and other rewards in the hope of securing their loyalty. We can also note, for future reference, that Richard's legal reforms had a strong moral and authoritarian tone. This raises the question of how ambitious and arrogant aristocrats may have reacted to the King's leadership. On one hand, they had the benefits of royal patronage, but on the other, his legislation threatened to further restrain their opportunistic tendencies in the pursuit of power and money.

During this same period, Richard suffered misfortune and mounting isolation, both politically and domestically. His son Edward, who was apparently a weakly child, died in April 1484. This was a severe blow. The *Crowland Chronicler*[35] recorded: '*You might have seen his father and mother in a state almost bordering on madness, by reason of their sudden grief*'. Queen Anne herself died of tuberculosis just a year later. These developments can have done nothing for Richard's state of mind and will have added to his concerns, since his legacy was now at risk. Politically, Richard's problem seemed twofold. First, since the revolt which included Buckingham's betrayal, Henry Tudor had become the agreed candidate around which Lancastrian sympathies gathered. Henry's claim to the throne may have been weak, but the settlement upon a single pretender added considerable power and influence to the Lancastrian cause.

35 The *Crowland Chronicle* was completed in about 1486 by an unknown writer who probably had first-hand knowledge of the events recorded. He was generally critical of Richard III's actions, but with Henry VII already on the throne, this is perhaps not particularly surprising.

Second, by this stage, there was a widespread belief that Richard had killed his nephews, and, even by 15th-century standards, this was felt by many to have been a step too far. Not only did this fuel the Lancastrian cause, it also divided the Yorkist establishment. The result was that Richard had insufficient support, particularly in the south of England, to administer his realm. His solution – to bring more and more northerners down to fulfil these roles – only served to isolate Richard further from the people upon whom he would need to rely to sustain his monarchy. Richard's loss of an heir and a queen only further weakened an increasingly insecure throne.

The matter of securing his succession was settled reasonably quickly upon the Earl of Lincoln, the son of his sister Elizabeth and the Duke of Suffolk. Other problems proved harder to resolve, and would not go away. The need for a new wife and direct heirs was never resolved in the time remaining to him, and it was to get him into more difficulty. At one point, the court flowed with rumours of his intention to marry his niece Elizabeth – some even suggesting that he was planning this whilst his wife was still alive. This is unlikely to have been true – to have married Elizabeth would have been to contradict the claim that Edward IV's children were illegitimate. Therefore, if he were to marry Elizabeth, he would be defining himself as a usurper. Whatever his intentions actually were, he was forced to deny the rumours publicly. The incident reveals a degree of disenchantment about Richard's monarchy and also reflects how isolated a figure Richard had become: after all, the male line in his family was now all but extinct and many of his former close associates were dead. Overall, the impression is that the standing of his monarchy was in decline: for as long as he had difficulty dispelling accusations of usurpation and infanticide, he was becoming increasingly vulnerable to the undermining effect of ongoing and vindictive rumour.

From spring 1485 onwards, Richard's energies were directed at countering the clear threat that Henry Tudor would risk invasion in that year. The enterprise looked extremely risky, but Henry was running out of time with his credit abroad and the sponsors of his cause. Richard can be expected to have taken the threat seriously but should have felt reasonably confident, on past experience, of seeing him off: he was an experienced general and had the resources of the monarchy behind him. That said, what is also obvious in hindsight is that he did not have the unquestioning loyalty of the noble families upon whom he was relying.

The invasion came on August 7th at Milford Haven, Pembrokeshire. The rest is well-known history. Finally encountering Henry's forces at Market Bosworth on August 22nd, the battle was not straightforward, with various factions of dubious loyalty distributed around the battlefield. Henry Percy, Duke of Northumberland, and commander of a large element of Richard's army, remained inactive nearby while events unfolded. It may be that there was no room for Percy's troops on the battlefield, and Richard decided not to deploy them immediately. However, what was seen as a betrayal by Richard's friends in the North was neither forgotten nor forgiven, and a few years later Percy was murdered by a mob near Thirsk.

Elsewhere on the field, Stanley did worse than simply stand by. He had hedged his bets throughout the campaign, and is alleged to have said that 'he had more sons', when Richard finally threatened to execute his son during the battle if he did not commit his support. Had Richard won, Stanley would, in all probability, have found a way to justify his actions. However, at the critical moment, seeing Richard's famous cavalry charge towards Henry Tudor's personal retinue, Stanley intervened in Henry Tudor's favour. Thus, with dying shouts of 'treason', Richard was overwhelmed. Much good did it do Stanley. In 1495, he was executed for treasonable dealings with the pretender Perkin Warbeck. *Plus ca change, plus c'est la meme chose*: the Tudor accession did not immediately change the attitudes of the aristocracy to the monarchy.

These are the (largely agreed) facts of Richard's life, although these are sparse enough. So sparse, indeed, that major questions such as the fate of Edward IV's sons have never been resolved, and understanding the motivations of individuals within this story sometimes strains the imagination. Why, for example, did the dowager Queen Elizabeth release her daughters into Richard's care from sanctuary in 1484 if he was believed to have murdered her sons? No subsequent account of their mistreatment is to be heard – and we can be sure that if there were any, the Tudors would have recorded it. How and why did Rivers and the others allow Richard to take control of Edward V at Stony Stratford? Why did Buckingham revolt against Richard and espouse Henry Tudor's cause? These simple questions amongst many tell us that the facts and narratives of Richard's life are simply incomplete.

A Timeline for 1483

9 April	Edward IV dies.
Mid-April	Richard is advised of Edward IV's death and leaves Middleham on about 20th April.
26 April	Richard arrives in Nottingham and exchanges messages with Earl Rivers to meet in Northampton.
29 April	Richard arrives in Northampton to find Rivers and Edward V camped 14 miles south in Stony Stratford.
30 April	Earl Rivers meets Richard in Northampton, dines, and is then arrested overnight.
1 May	Richard rides to Stony Stratford and takes custody of Edward V. Rivers, Vaughan, and Grey are sent north to Sheriff Hutton and Pontefract for imprisonment.
2/3 May	The Dowager Queen Elizabeth, with Prince Richard of York and her daughters, takes sanctuary in Westminster Abbey. Edward IV's Treasury is stolen and the remaining Woodville family flees.
4 May	On receiving guarantees of safety, Richard and his entourage, including Edward V, enter London. Edward V is placed in the Tower of London for safe-keeping.
10 May	Richard recognised as Protector. Edward V's coronation is rescheduled for late June.
10 June	Richard writes to northern supporters to bring an army to London to come to his aid.

13 June	Hastings, Stanley, the Archbishop of York, and the Bishop of Ely are arrested at a meeting in the Tower of London, accused of treason. Hastings is immediately executed outside.
16 June	Queen Elizabeth releases Prince Richard, Duke of York, into the custody of Duke Richard the Protector, possibly coerced. Prince Richard joins his brother Edward V in the Tower of London.
22 June	Ralph Shaw preaches at St Paul's of the illegitimacy of Edward IV's sons and Richard of Gloucester's legitimate claim to the throne.
24 June	The Duke of Buckingham makes a speech to the same effect in the Guildhall.
25 June	Rivers, Vaughan, and Grey are executed at Pontefract whilst in London a collection of parliamentary nobles petition Richard to assume the throne.
26 June	Richard agrees to the petition and becomes King Richard III.
6 July	Richard crowned at Westminster.
July	The princes in the Tower are withdrawn from public sight and no further news is heard of them.
Late July	Richard leaves Windsor to progress through Reading, Oxford, Gloucester, Tewksbury, Worcester, Warwick (arriving August 8th), Coventry, Leicester, Nottingham, Pontefract, and York.

11 October   Travelling south and arriving at Lincoln, Richard hears of a rebellion, including the Duke of Buckingham.

2 November   Having been betrayed and captured, Buckingham is executed at Salisbury. The rebellion is crushed.

Chapter Seven

The unravelling:
Richard's state of mind: 1483–1485

The cliché '*when the going gets tough, the tough get going*' could reasonably be taken to imply that 'winners' are tougher than most. But it could also reflect the fact that winners tend to get to write the history and put their success down to their positive qualities rather than luck. Winston Churchill was honest (or self-aware) enough to declare this explicitly and proceeded to do the writing himself. Hindsight is equally distorting of failure. In the sense that he did not survive long as King, and that he died in battle, Richard failed. As a result, his defamation was inevitable. The question here is: how did his personality, and the decisions he made, contribute to this, and the reputational damage that followed? The approach in this book is to describe these last few years of Richard's life in terms of a coherent account of his psychology built up from his life before these events. This account – which we are assuming for the present is not based upon monstrous psychological abnormalities – then seeks to explain Richard's actions in the face of some extraordinarily challenging circumstances.

We should remember that these circumstances are extraordinary in two senses. First, there were decisions of enormous moment wrapped in a crisis of sheer survival. Some decisions were immediate, as in battle, but other crises unfolded more quietly over months and years, even if their consequences were equally deadly. Human beings, including kings in the 15th century, are fallible when dealing with such problems. Certainly, with kings, we may be looking at tested, experienced leaders. But they are still humans improvising novel solutions to existential threats. We should not be surprised at the odd extraordinary mistake and such mistakes cannot necessarily be taken as evidence of abnormal psychological processes.

The second sense in which the circumstances are extraordinary is that we have so little reliable observational evidence of how humans operate in these circumstances. Appropriate experiments cannot easily be conducted in our society, and even when they have been, questions remain. How 'realistic' did Milgram's and Zimbardo's experimental participants feel their situation was, or were they merely playing a part in what they knew to be an experiment? History suggests that these participants behave much as others have in real circumstances. For example, Nazi scientists felt able to conduct experiments that ended in the mutilation or death of their human participants. But this is not the same as Richard's position. He was born a leader of men, not a functionary within a society such as Nazi Germany, or a participant in Milgram's experiments – both situations where the human capacity to behave cruelly and aggressively can be explained by a willingness to submit to accepted authority. Applying what psychological theory we have to such singular circumstances has, therefore, to be done cautiously. The previous chapters described a formulation of Richard as an assertive authoritarian and discussed both how that character type is formed, and how well it fits his known behaviour up to 1483. On this basis, we now consider how Richard's version of 'ordinary psychology' confronted the consequences of his brother's death.

Throughout his adult life, and certainly after the death of his brother George, Richard must have speculated on what to do in the event of Edward IV's death. It seems reasonable to assume that it was not expected for some time. Certainly Edward IV himself had made little provision for it and appears unaware, until the last moment, of his imminent demise. Therefore Richard would probably have been anticipating that Edward V would assume the throne in full maturity, in which case the issue of Protectorship would not have arisen. This is not to say that Richard would welcome the change of monarch if, as seems likely, Edward V was strongly influenced by his Woodville relatives. So the issue of planning for the succession would have been on Richard's mind, as it would for any powerful political figure considering the future. However, the speed of onset of Edward IV's last illness and death must have taken Richard by surprise and it seems unlikely that he had specific plans for the circumstances that then presented themselves.

We can also be sure that Richard was aware of the threat that the Woodville family represented, even if the evidence that he was already hostile towards them is meagre. As it was, resentment in Edward's court was already rife. Offices, power, and lands were preferred upon the Woodvilles, and their daughters were imposed as wives upon status-conscious nobles such as the Duke of Buckingham. However diplomatic he might have been, Richard's views about this were probably also common knowledge or common surmise. At the very least, some degree of wariness and suspicion between Richard and the Woodville affinity was to be expected. Once Richard had taken possession of Edward V's person and made for London, these sentiments were amplified: the Woodvilles either scattered or made for sanctuary. Obviously, they were not confident of Richard's generosity towards them. Equally, in writing to summon aid from York on June 11th 1483, Richard did not mix his words when he referred to 'the queen, her blood adherents and affinity… intended… to murder us… by their damnable ways.' But by then, of course, matters had escalated.

On first hearing the news of Edward IV's death, Richard would have taken some time to muster forces before moving south. In this time, we can assume that the machinations in court, and those of the Woodville family in particular, would be uppermost in his mind, and that he would be receiving news of their developing plans and actions by letter. His first response was to send appropriate letters of reassurance, fealty, and regard for Edward V's well-being. One supposes they represented due process and no one would read much into them. Certainly there would be no point in doing anything more antagonistic at this stage. However, it seems likely that he intended to intercept Edward V and take control of his person as soon as possible. Consider the alternative: it is possible to imagine someone in his position joining Rivers and Edward V at Northampton and accompanying them to London. The calculation would then be as follows: there, as Protector, he would hope to be able to exert enough influence upon the Council and upon Edward V himself to effect a peaceful transition to a new reign as Edward reached maturity.

But there were at least two or three problems with this from Richard's point of view. First, the strategy was risky and any conciliatory approaches on his part could render him more vulnerable if his rivals did not operate in good faith. Nor could he be sure of his ability to impose himself on events if he needed to: the Dowager Queen and her retinue were rivals who could be expected to use their influence in Council to its full. Nor could Richard rely upon the goodwill of Edward V who, in all likelihood, would align with his maternal family. Second, and critically for this analysis, this strategy admitted no foreseeable closure. Even if it were to succeed, Richard would need to be involved, in some capacity or other, in a regency lasting some years, during which time there would be an ever-present threat and from which he personally stood to gain relatively little for the risk involved. The historical precedents of previous regencies were not good.

Given what we now believe about Richard's character, these uncertainties and risks would be unacceptable. It would be much more consistent for him to come to a decision to be proactive and to maximise his sense of personal control immediately. For him, the decision has the advantage of immediate closure and of the removal of a considerable degree of uncertainty. He would realise that failure might be disastrous but equally that his destruction would anyway follow later if he did not act. By this stage in his life, and in the face of a clear and present danger, Richard's predisposition would favour assertive action.

I add a third possible motivation. We have to accept the possibility that Richard did not want Edward V to assume the monarchy and that he very much wanted it for himself. It has been fashionable to think – perhaps because it exonerates Richard from an accusation of calculating his usurpation from the very start – that his assumption of the crown was forced upon him by a cascade of events, of which his encounter with Rivers and Edward V at Stony Stratford was one of the first. By this account, each of these events were motivated by immediate necessity rather than conforming to a long-term goal, but which, as the story unfolded and he 'learned' of the bastardy of the princes, ultimately made assumption of the throne unavoidable.

Such an account almost makes Richard a victim of circumstance, and it suits people sympathetic to Richard to believe this. But the psychology suggests otherwise. In the years preceding Edward IV's death, we see Richard assiduously building up his power and, as we have observed, he could be ruthless in this. He could even – although it runs against the received wisdom of him – play fast and loose with the law to get what he wanted. His psychology, from his earliest years, was motivated by the need for security, to overcome threats, and to reinforce his self-esteem in the process. This constant need is accompanied by the vicious and destructive irony that the self-same psychology operates as an early-warning system to detect threat. Richard's authoritarian and controlling personality was accompanied by a heightened degree of anxiety bordering upon paranoia. But then this was the later 15th century, and one could argue that what might be considered paranoid now was merely prudent then. To digress briefly, Richard's need to reinforce his self-esteem might also explain why he was assiduous in the matter of self-serving propaganda, as observed by several historians. The received wisdom that he played a central role in battles such as Barnet and Tewksbury is not represented in independent chronicles and may rest, in part, in accounts Richard wished to be circulated.

Returning to the hypothesis that Richard had ambitions for the throne himself, the crux of Richard's thinking in this case would boil down to yet more binary questions, the key word being 'binary', as in 'yes or no' or 'right and wrong'. As discussed in earlier chapters, the psychology here is to remove uncertainty and complexity and replace this with absolutes. Additionally, as a process of resolving cognitive dissonance, or at least of solving problems, it is usual for one alternative to be one with which the individual is totally aligned and the other to be one easy to reject. These binary alternatives are not usually arrived at by logical analysis and must be seen ultimately as self-serving. Questions Richard might pose to himself could include: am I the most powerful person in the realm, or is my brother's son? And who would be the better king? If he asked himself these questions – and it is hard to imagine he did not – it is unimaginable that he would not choose himself over his nephew. The only obstacle to this rests with Edward's legitimacy as Edward IV's rightful heir, and Richard would not find it impossible to dismantle this line of argument in his mind: in terms of his power, Edward was as yet completely unproven, and the taint of his Woodville inheritance was a significant deterrent. If, additionally, there was any hint of questioning the legitimacy of Edward V's succession, then from Richard's point of view he was himself both the right man for the job and the legitimate heir.

It is possible that, at the point of taking control of Edward V, Richard may not have been entirely honest even with himself over these questions. That act bought him time to see how circumstances developed, and natural caution would review, a step at a time, how to proceed. But psychology tells us that, except in the most unusual circumstances (such as mathematical analysis), we solve problems by entertaining the preferred solution and working backwards. Therefore it is inconceivable that someone with Richard's psychology – an admixture of caution and planning coupled with a very strong sense of his own destiny – would not have explored the possibility of becoming king himself. This does not mean he was either committed to it at this stage (although it would have taken quite extraordinary circumstances for Richard subsequently to sublimate his own interests in favour of Edward V[36]), or that he had planned the process by which it would happen in detail. But it is in the nature of someone like Richard to put himself in that position. There is no evidence to suggest that Richard had the intellectual detachment to do otherwise, and the sanctity of the royal succession would not have been sufficient motivation to overcome his own self-protecting assertiveness, particularly if any plausible question mark over the legitimacy of succession was in play.

Returning from that speculation of Richard's motivations, we might therefore see his taking control of Edward V at Stony Stratford as entirely predictable. Perhaps the more surprising element in this is that Richard (accompanied by Buckingham) actually managed to pull off the coup of taking control of Edward V in the face of a larger force. Circumstances may have favoured him. Rivers may not have been as cautious as he might have been. His arrival at Northampton allowed Richard and Buckingham to isolate him from the force he

36 Note also that, by the so-called confirmation bias, the cognitive system would be more receptive to any subsequent evidence that supported his direction of travel and was less sensitive to the opposite. Once he had taken these early decisions, there is a natural acceleration in the likelihood that his ultimate goal of usurpation would be followed through.

was commanding. The following morning, when Richard and Buckingham had ridden to Stony Stratford, Grey and Vaughan are also presented with a ticklish problem: Rivers had already been arrested and they may have realised that opposing, or offering violence to, the two most senior dukes in the realm was too drastic a responsibility to undertake. They would be aware that their faction had uncertain support in the country. Either way, they submitted to arrest and their forces – by all accounts larger than Richard's entourage – were dispersed without dissent.

Grey and Vaughan's reluctance to commit themselves to any resistance allowed Richard to assert his authority. His response is unsubtle and pre-emptory, and, if this is a correct account of what happened, vindictive and escalatory. Along with Rivers, Grey and Vaughan are immediately sent north for imprisonment. As soon as he arrives in London, Richard presses for their execution. Why? Richard claimed that they had intended to murder him, but the evidence is circumstantial at best and his claim is just as likely to represent a means to an end. It could be seen as calculated political opportunism in which the aim is to remove significantly powerful enemies and to cow opposition elsewhere. But even if that aim is a reasonable one, there is more to this. As discussed in an earlier chapter, one effect of stress and anxiety is to constrain the decision-making process. Moderation and any acceptance of uncertainty is supplanted by absolutism. Tried-and-tested solutions come to the fore. For an authoritarian such as Richard, whose early psychology increases his sensitivity to threat, he is therefore far more likely to interpret a protagonist's behaviour as a direct threat and more likely to seek extreme remedies. The complex is turned into the absolutely simple. The historical record is silent on this point, but this episode suggests that Richard is not just making political calculations dispassionately: under a degree of stress, the vindictive and authoritarian elements of his character came to the fore.

Ross's history of Richard describes the next few weeks as 'meagerly reported' in contemporary chronicles. This may be because so much manoeuvring was taking place behind the scenes, or perhaps because there was good reason to think, from any chronicler's point of view, that discretion was the better part of valour. The less committed to record, the better. Nevertheless, there is some evidence of Richard overly favouring his closest associates at this time (including Buckingham) as his Protectorship took on the authority of the Crown. This offers a reason why Hastings, amongst others, may have been willing to be party to a Woodville-based conspiracy as these central characters of Edward IV's monarchy felt preference and power slipping away from them. It is not clear whether substantive evidence will ever be found for such a conspiracy, but it is highly plausible. Also, as early as late May 1483, some of the contemporary records indicate suspicions that Richard intended to take the crown himself. It must have been transparent to all that Richard must, at the very least, have been considering the possibility. Given his power and any momentum in that direction, we can see that senior figures in the Council who did not relish the possibility would need to take steps sooner rather than later to avert it. The inevitable crisis, if such it was, breaks at the meeting at which Hastings was summarily arrested and executed.

This incident, on Friday June 13th, confirms a darker view of Richard's state of mind and we have to consider whether it represented an outburst or was part of a planned process. It is tempting to explore the possibility that this violence stemmed from uncontrolled aggression. This can occur in cautious and over-controlled individuals (as is consistent with our formulation of Richard) if they are driven by circumstances to the point where their ability to repress negative thoughts is lost, at which point a flood of unfettered aggression follows. Thus, in this scenario, after a long period of tension, Richard loses control on discovering the disloyalty of a previously trusted colleague. Sentimental arguments could follow that Richard's regret for this emotional lapse leads him to make what amends he can by supporting Hastings' widow and arranging his burial alongside Edward IV, as previously requested. The problem with this account is that the facts do not correspond with modern theories of over-controlled aggression. Here, the key element is that the individual experiences an explosion of uncontrolled violence once their ability to control and inhibit their aggressive behaviour is lost. Had this been the case, it would have been more in character for Richard suddenly to have run amok and murder Hastings himself in a fit of blind rage. This did not occur. The facts much better fit an act of a premeditated ambush (possibly set up by the device of timetabling two separate innocuous meetings simultaneously) in which Hastings and the others were caught unawares by armed men who were already at hand to arrest the councillors at a given signal.

This therefore looks very much like a calculated act of realpolitik designed to head off a Woodville-led conspiracy. The death of Hastings and then, soon after, the executions of Rivers, Vaughan, and Grey were the price to pay for Richard's authority to be established. In the short term, the price would seem quite low. After all, in comparison, Henry VII's accession to the throne tallied up a much larger headcount (perhaps an unfortunate, although apposite, phrase!). But Henry's position was less ambiguous, and on this occasion the result of decision-making under stress seems rather more obvious. For Richard, in fact, the price was probably too high in the long run: in destroying Hastings, Richard was escalating the sense of crisis in London and alienating that element of the establishment who stood for continuity, and specifically not necessarily for the Woodville interest. In the interests of a stable Protectorship, this turned out to be a poor strategy. But in the short-term pursuance of a coup d'etat it makes more sense. If Richard intended to be King, he had to risk his hand in a gambler's move. The longer he worked for a stable and consensual Protectorship, the momentum for Edward V eventually to succeed in his own right would increase, and any support and opportunity Richard had for his own accession would diminish. Further, any legal claim he might fabricate would lose traction; threats to his person from other ambitious men would always be present; and the disapproval that a delayed usurpation would attract would increase to the point that his monarchy would be weakened from the onset.

In May and June 1483, Richard had two choices: either he worked with the existing Council to ensure Edward V's smooth accession – a strategy that would seem to him to be fraught with risk both in the short and long term – or he aimed for the throne himself. Hasting's execution must therefore signal a decision towards the latter. Either it denotes the breakdown of any hope he might have had to secure his own safety under Edward V's monarchy (reflecting a change of strategy to usurp the throne himself), or it reveals that he was already aiming in that direction and responded when Hastings and the others represented an obstacle. From the point of view of the psychological formulation made here, the possibility that Richard was conducting his Protectorship in good faith seems more unlikely. Richard would neither be able to tolerate the long-term risk and uncertainty it would entail. Nor would he be able to suppress his own ambitions based upon his own self-worth. As Ross puts it, the removal of Hastings made Richard's bid for the throne irreversible. It is likely that he had already made up his mind to that effect.

The remaining events leading up to his coronation in early July are then entirely consistent with a coordinated strategy of usurpation. There may or may not have been some substance to the claim that Edward IV's marriage was void, making it possible for Richard to stake a claim himself, but it feels implausible to imagine that Bishop Stillington just happened to volunteer evidence at precisely the right time. Indeed, so many different accounts of Edward V's illegitimacy seem to have been current (including Edward IV's bastardy and Edward IV's proxy marriage with a French princess, as well as the claim that he was pre-contracted to Lady Eleanor Butler) that it is much more likely that Richard simply chose one that he thought he could make work. There is no evidence to lead us to think that Richard either believed or disbelieved these stories. But in a sense, that judgement is irrelevant: his mentality would by now be entirely committed to a successful assumption of the throne. Any sense in his mind of the rightness of this act is based on his assessment of himself as the most suitable king, rather than the provenance of the 'facts' that serve as a means to that end.

If Richard knew that Stillington's evidence was fabricated, and given what he had already done, he might have had some serious cognitive dissonance to resolve. He wanted to be king at the same time as a powerless boy – his nephew, no less – had a stronger legal claim. On that basis, Richard's psychology would seek to bolster his own claim while diminishing that of Edward V. We can never know what the basis of that resolution would have been in Richard's mind, but, there is no reason to think that the mechanisms to resolve that dissonance were any different from those we all use to resolve our more petty issues. Some candidates suggest themselves:

1. In comparison to Edward V, Richard saw himself as the more powerful and experienced individual. Without doubt, he was the more qualified to rule the kingdom;

2. The Kingdom needed a strong leader with the authority to manage the political uncertainties in place, not least the enmities and tension left by Edward's favouring of the Woodvilles;

3. Whether or not Edward V was illegitimate (and remembering that psychological biases would make it more likely for Richard to believe that he was, even without the hard evidence), Edward V's affinity to the Woodville family would make his accession unacceptable to Richard. For the purposes of resolving internal conflict, Richard might well have redefined the term 'illegitimate' to include 'born a Woodville'.

One can perhaps think of other, or alternative, formulations of these ideas. The point is that Richard was able to resolve his cognitive dissonance and is likely to have done it in a way which emphasised the rightness of his decision for both himself and the realm. A different psychology might get to the same position without the same sense of seeking the moral high ground. Such a person would hold the whole of society in contempt, declaring to themselves that they had 'won' or 'got away with it' (to use modern parlance) as motivation and reward for what they had done. For reasons discussed in the next chapter, such a character would be verging towards the psychopathic. The next chapter describes at length why this is unlikely to describe Richard. Pathological motivations need constant feeding with reward. The psychopath in this situation would not then be able to get down to the day-to-day business of governance – something Richard did assiduously – without seeking further reward by further demonstrations of contempt.

The next thing we have to consider is the fate of his two nephews in the tower. No evidence has emerged, or is likely to emerge, that will resolve this issue unambiguously. The question for this book is whether a psychological perspective has anything to add. By the time their last appearances are recorded, Richard had experienced Buckingham's rebellion. The risk that opposing factions might use them in the future against Richard's monarchy was a real and present danger. The simple logic – borne out of numerous examples over the previous 100 years – was that this risk could only be eliminated with the disappearance of the princes. Apologists for Richard might suggest he somehow secreted them away to secure their well-being in obscurity, but it simply doesn't add up as a safe strategy. Nor was Richard a sufficiently creative or particularly compassionate man to carry out such an innovation. He was, of his times, a conservative authoritarian, and historical precedent only pointed in one direction. It is true that these were minors nominally under his protection, and equally true that this fact would subsequently be used against him as opposition to his reign gained momentum, but it doesn't alter the logic that would have driven Richard to eliminate them.

In this, we must also consider Richard's response to continuing political instability and opposition to his monarchy. The events of summer 1483 were divisive. He had thoroughly wrong-footed his opponents both in seizing Edward, and then by Hastings' execution. This made his subsequent progression to kingship unstoppable. But it was a process that did nothing to endear him to those whose support he would need afterwards. However, if the analysis of Richard's character is correct, his personality was forged in the face of adversity from his earliest years, and was based on his self-resilience in the face of opposition. He may not have liked the difficulties he experienced in 1483, but he was not a man to back off when he encountered them. His instinct was to act and to continue to be in control of the situation if at all possible. This being the case, the princes were doomed. Richard, like most decision-makers, chose to deal with simple logic.

This simplicity of logic is the means by which any pang of guilt or doubt he might have experienced is resolved. Richard had come this far, and he was now the rightful King anointed by God. His duty was now to continue in that fashion. In this situation, duty wore the same clothes as cold-hearted doggedness and inflexibility. That anyone was seeking to use these boys to challenge his position meant that they, and not he, were responsible for their fate. To summarise, we cannot know for certain if Richard felt guilt (on the assumption he was responsible for their deaths), or by which logic he justified his position to himself. But it is possible to demonstrate how readily the decision to kill his nephews would come to such a determined mind in a time when such brutal logic was commonplace. Equally, and in an argument that applies also to Hasting's execution, such a determined mind comes from discounting the uncertainty of what might happen afterwards.

That is how our minds work to make these decisions possible at all. However, the clear difference between 'ordinary' decision-makers (that is, ourselves) and Richard is that, for most of us, few decisions are of such consequence. For Richard, on the other hand, the decisions he made at the beginning of his monarchy caused difficulties until the end of his life, and almost certainly hastened it.

After the 1483 rebellion, Richard's reign continued for another two years. Since this is not an historical account of that time, I do not concentrate upon the minutiae of his government, preferring to focus upon incidents or revelations that give further insight into Richard's psychological make-up. The first thing to note is that Richard applied himself to government assiduously. Ross, for example, describes him as 'an energetic and efficient King', and this view is repeated by other historians and contemporary commentaries. He seems to have achieved much in the time he had. This in itself is revealing insofar as it is entirely consistent with our formulation of a controlled, dutiful man who saw his destiny as a 'good' king and sought to realise it. As argued earlier, a more capricious psychopath whose primary motivation was to exercise power for his own gratification would have found the workload, and the attention to detail Richard was known for, unattractive, favouring more extravagant gestures. We will explore this possibility further in the next chapter.

Richard certainly had work to do, some of which proved too long-term to complete in the remaining time allocated to him. The rebellion of 1483 generated a political vacuum in the south of England as so many of the local aristocrats rose against him. Although few lost their lives, many more fled to France to support Henry Tudor's claim to the throne, and those remaining could not be trusted to administer his wishes. Richard's response was a wholesale influx of northerners to take their place. This was an undesirable consequence because the county establishments were better geared to management by local interests: the whole hierarchy of patronage depended upon it. The problem continued for the rest of Richard's reign. Richard was also chronically short of money and the disruption to the normal governance did nothing to assist the raising of funds. Finally, the incidental effect of the 1483 rebellion was to strengthen Henry Tudor's hand as more and more landowners saw him as a plausible alternative to Richard. Consequently, Richard was preoccupied with the defence of the realm and conducting foreign policy to the same end. But it is perhaps telling, and entirely consistent with a view of Richard as a persistent and controlling personality, that he maintained a sense of diligence in the face of this adversity. This propensity to persist – again a characteristic of controlling personalities – may mean that tasks are achieved through perseverance, but it can just as easily result in failure through inflexibility. Where others might have adopted lateral, perhaps more pragmatic, strategies, Richard continued to dig in and try harder with strategies that were not working.

During this time, Richard is also described in historical accounts as a conventional monarch, again entirely consistent with his conservative character. He shows the same taste as his brother in fashionable display at court, including fine clothes and a reputation for musical excellence. He also initiated many plans for building and for scholastic and religious foundations. In law, he placed particular emphasis upon proper conduct and justice and, while his foreign policy was ultimately unable to contain the threat of Henry Tudor, there is no sense in which it can be described as disastrous. Again, to paraphrase Ross, it is hard to find fault in his conduct of government during his reign.

And yet Richard's travails remained. It seems clear that he was unable to restore stability and order to the satisfaction of the country as a whole. Polydor Vergil[37] claimed that Richard had been widely disliked even when he put up a show of being a 'good king'. In pointing out that Richard was the only usurper in the

37   Polydor Vergil (1470–1555). An Italian cleric and chronicler of English
       history who spent most of his life after 1504 in England. His recollections
       of public opinion are therefore first hand.

Middle Ages who failed to consolidate his throne in the longer term, Horrox lists converging reasons for this. These include: there being no accepted dissatisfaction with the previous regime because Edward V, by definition, was completely untainted in this respect; a narrow, northern-weighted powerbase; no 'sanction of military victory' whereby winning a critical battle was seen as a form of endorsement; and, perhaps most important of all, the means by which Richard seized power and disposed of his nephews had divided and repelled a substantial portion of the existing Yorkist establishment. The inability to be seen as any improvement on the previous regime without any positive endorsement of his contribution could only result in his being seen as a change for the worse.

As hinted above, some of Richard's difficulties in overcoming these problems of credibility in his reign lay in his own personality. Based on a mindset of resilience whose foundations lay in childhood, Richard can be characterised as a controlled and controlling individual. His authoritarian attitudes, a firm belief in justice and retribution, and a strong piety, all point in the direction of deeply established coping strategies designed to defend his self-esteem from an incipient insecurity. Other fragments and clues available to us are consistent with this. For example, his prayer book contained prayers asking to be freed from 'tribulations, griefs and anguishes which I face'. These may have been added after the death of his son or his wife, but they also reflect a generally embattled personality. We have also to note a recurrent and aggressive use of character assassination as a means of manipulating public opinion against his enemies. This was often linked with public pronouncements to be vigilant against debauchery and vice, identifying the Woodvilles and Henry Tudor's followers as particular sinners. Finally, we can note Richard's use of the most severe punishments in an attempt to discourage treasonable behaviour in the run-up to Henry Tudor's invasion. All of this, coupled with an attention to detail that many of the more ambitious and self-regarding nobles would have found tiresome (if not threatening) when aimed at them, paints a picture of someone determined to maintain control at all costs and with little latitude or willingness to be more pragmatic. This is again characteristic of a fundamentally insecure, controlling personality and it does not appear to have been mitigated in other ways. For example, his coterie of close, loyal associates was very small, and he was so concerned that others, like Stanley, whose support he had bought with gifts, might yet defect, that he took to keeping his son as a hostage. This feels more like a mentality of siege.

In this climate, Richard's now-proven scoliosis has to be taken more seriously than has been previously considered. In an earlier chapter, we saw that any visible evidence of it would have acted in subtle ways both upon Richard and upon his interlocutors. At this stage in his life, with the reputation of having killed both Hastings and Edward IV's sons (amongst others), no one could feel entirely safe. A degree of caution in their dealings with the King was therefore to be expected, especially since he had demonstrated the ability to strike fast and without warning. Consequently, any additional impediment to the smooth flow of social intercourse would have a disproportionate effect. When two people are speaking, if one feels uncomfortable for whatever reason, or the conversation feels awkward, the discomfort increases on both sides. That discomfort is a breeding ground for negative attribution. The underlying purpose of that attribution is to provide a satisfactory explanation for one's own discomfort in terms of characteristics of the other person's personality. In this way, fault lies with the other person and one's own self-esteem is protected. Therefore, assuming the scoliosis was evident, it would influence the normal flow of social interaction, and its effect on Richard would be significant.

Quite how negative is hard to judge. The assessment of Richard's skeleton led to the conclusions that he probably had an ordinary gait and that any asymmetry between his shoulder heights could have been largely concealed by adjustments to clothing. Richard was not grotesque, but some asymmetry was visible to Rous as a contemporary commentator, although we should remember that he was not an unbiased witness. On the other hand, when one reads accounts such as Von Poppelau's extended visit to Middleham in May 1484 as an ambassador, no comment of that kind is made, even though Poppelau provides a physical description of Richard. We may also note that Poppelau's dealings with Richard did not seem to be awkward; he referred to Richard as being most gracious towards him. But then we are dealing with a foreign visitor who would have no reason to be suspicious or cautious in Richard's company, any more than Richard would have been wary of him. Overall, one assumes that Richard's scoliosis was relatively insignificant and one suspects in anyone else it would have little impact upon their social interactions in an immediate sense. However, by this stage, Richard is not 'anyone else': he is a man with an unpleasant record and whose future was uncertain whilst Henry Tudor's claim to the throne was gaining traction. Ultimately, men of substance around him were aware that they may have to make a choice between supporting Richard or an alternative. In this context, relatively minor issues such as physical deformity, social stiffness, or an unusually fussy and controlling personality (as perceived by others) begin to take narrative weight that tip the balance of their decisions in one direction rather than another, quite in the same manner that many a petition for acrimonious divorce might end up being expressed in terms of how the partner chewed their breakfast cereal.

From the outset, Richard might have hoped to have overcome the many reasons people had to be unhappy with his assumption of power, especially if he felt that by grasping the reins of power and offering a strong and stable government on Edward's death would be what most of the nobility desired at the end of the 15th century. But this was not enough. If polled individually, a great number of the aristocracy might well have agreed, at the end of a very difficult century, that this is precisely what was needed. They might also, according to the attitudes of the times, have conceded that the odd casualty – such as Hastings and even royal princes – was an acceptable, if harsh, price to pay. But that does not mean that this view would emerge as the consensus. Coherent, like-minded groups (as was the Yorkist establishment that Richard most divided and offended) are capable of an aberration that has been described as 'groupthink'. What is interesting about this social phenomenon is that it runs in the face of the common belief that when groups of people form a collective opinion, extreme views are averaged out to produce a middle-of-the-road consensus. In fact, where social groups share loyalty and basic principles, numerous studies have shown that the attitudes and decisions emerging from them drift towards extreme, rather than average, positions. This is the result of a process in which the coherence of the group's values is given greater weight than a dispassionate analysis of the facts at hand[38], and one that we now see today in the echo chambers of social media.

Such a process is incremental but accelerating, because views are likely to be repeated and rehearsed within a social group and eventually become established as received wisdom. Thus for Richard a critical period would have been the very beginning of the crisis of 1483, where negative and positive attributes might equally have been voiced, and where there might have been some uncertainty before an accepted wisdom reached a tipping point that established a consensus either way. In this, Richard's operational effectiveness during his usurpation may well have served against him in the longer term. One suspects that few believed the story of Edward's pre-contract with Eleanor Butler – it wasn't even the first story that was floated. That said, in similar circumstances other leaders have got away with more outrageous

---

38 Groupthink was first discussed and investigated by Irving Janis (*Victims of Groupthink*, 1972, New York: Houghton Mifflin). It has been described as a plausible basis of disasters such as the Bay of Pigs invasion and the loss of the *Challenger* spacecraft.

lies. However, by this stage, with Richard in complete control of the royal princes, Hastings dead, the Woodville family dispersed or in sanctuary, and a potentially hostile army just north of London, no one was in a position to oppose him. Richard coerced his way to the throne and he was unfortunate in the sense that he was neither able to represent it as a victory in battle, nor justifiable on the basis of replacing a corrupt regime.

Any resentment this would predictably have generated may be the starting point which leads to Richard being unliked by the Yorkist establishment and the rise in Henry Tudor's prospects, but it was probably not the only cause. In this study we are interested in examining a plausible, 'normal' psychological perspective on this process. Historians have suggested that, given time, Richard may have turned this situation around, as did Henry VII after him (or at least to the point that he left a stable regime for Henry VIII to inherit). However, if the formulation of Richard's personality in this book is remotely correct, this may not have been possible. In such a view, Richard's death at Bosworth was a natural culmination of an increasing decline in the public perception of him that, had it not ended there, would have led to something similar in due course. In this view, the key aspects of Richard's personality would have continued to drive a wedge between himself and his desired aim of being seen as a 'good lord' (to borrow Horrox's label) by others.

To summarise, the characteristics of Richard's personality described here as instrumental in his ultimate downfall are all, in themselves, quite modest and considered quite 'normal' in the sense that they are seen in many of us in the present day. This includes Richard holding clear views about the structure of society and the enactment of justice, and an assertiveness in his own interest that could be threatening if he himself felt threatened. He could be appear vindictive and he could be difficult to divert from chosen paths of action, believing himself to be in the right and possibly a man of destiny. And he could work very hard, with much attention to detail, to get his own way. These are all qualities, in moderation, that mark important and influential people. But, if in any way seen in excess, or seen in circumstances where the outcome could be regarded as excessive (as in the death of the royal princes), perceptions change fundamentally and the same characteristics are seen as evidence of an overly controlling personality. To some extent such control is essential in a leader – by definition. But rather in the way Richard controlled his assumption of power, it is a mechanism that can leave others feeling disempowered and vulnerable if carried too forcefully. Had Richard engendered those feelings in the magnates of the country such as Buckingham, Percy, and Stanley, it would not be at all surprising for them to feel threatened by it, since it was the sine qua non for the leader of any major family at the time to seek to extend their dynastic power, not to see it diminished by the King. Inflexible and threatening, Richard may not have been a king they thought they could do business with.

Henry Tudor's fortunes after the rebellion of 1483 improved significantly, to the point where he was accepted as the de facto pretender to the throne. The presence of this threat – or opportunity, as seen by many – served to keep the heat under the debate as to whether Richard was or was not to be supported. In a climate in which the ingredients of groupthink are being stewed, this means that relatively minor irritants in Richard's personality, such as some possible problems with social interaction, a degree of vindictiveness, and his reliance on a small, inner circle of trust (with an implied degree of distrust to the others) will gain disproportionate significance. Furthermore, Richard's loss of support would inevitably be inversely related to Henry Tudor's gain. This leads to the speculation that any disconnect between him and the people whose loyalty he ultimately needed to consolidate his reign widened, rather than narrowed, over time. If that is true, a calamity of some kind, if not at Bosworth, was surely inevitable.

Richard's final charge at Bosworth in the attempt to destroy Henry Tudor seems entirely in character. He saw a chance and took it. He acted rather than waited, and it would have been entirely against his character to have withdrawn from the field possibly to fight again another day. The thing he most sought was closure at the earliest moment. After all, he might well have succeeded. He died presumably because Stanley saw a better future with a grateful Henry VII as king than with the king he knew. If this analysis is correct, Richard was a fairly ordinary man with some distinctive features of character which can be clustered around the idea of a controlling personality founded on the need to defend a basic sense of insecurity in childhood. He was not a monster or anything like it. What was extraordinary were the circumstances in which he found himself in 1483. As has already been remarked, had he died in that year rather than Edward IV, he would have been a relatively unremarkable footnote in history. In the event, he was faced with a difficult situation and he did what he thought was best for himself: and probably justified it by arguing it was best for the nation as well. The usurpation of the throne was executed efficiently – possibly too efficiently. The personality that hitherto worked well for him as Lord of the North was not suited to sustain him, under the circumstances by which he attained it, in kingship. This was not two different men, but the same man in two very different circumstances separated by a few weeks of life-changing activity whose consequences could be neither undone nor forgotten. He probably could not have behaved differently, and in that sense, Richard was simultaneously the victim and the villain of the piece. To attempt to paint him as one without the other is to fail to recognise his humanity and the pressure extraordinary circumstances place upon any human being.

Chapter Eight

Richard the Psychopath?

Within three months of Edward IV's death, his son Edward V had been supplanted, four significant nobles had been executed, others imprisoned, and Richard III had assumed the throne. Whether this represents a coup or realpolitik, it was bound to attract accusations of Richard having murdered his way to the top. Further executions and the disappearance of the princes only served to reinforce that suspicion. In such a short reign, Richard was also denied a period during which 'spin' and manufactured hindsight might have softened the perceived ruthlessness of his accession, as was arguably the case with Henry VII. In different circumstances, posterity might have been more kind to Richard.

As it happened, it was relatively easy for the Tudors to portray Richard as the Machiavellian monster we are shown in Shakespeare's tragedy. But is there any evidence for this? In the complex mix of Tudor propaganda and historical accounts of Richard's life, this accusation has clung closely to Richard and it lurks in the background of any historical analysis. We need therefore to consider what is usually meant by describing someone as a psychopathic killer, and whether it applies to Richard III. Specifically, having examined Richard's character, and looked at what we might describe as 'normal' processes of judgement and decision-making, we can ask what further evidence it would take for us to draw the conclusion that he was some form of psychopath.

The term 'psychopath' is perhaps misunderstood because specific kinds of psychopaths (usually portrayed in the form of serial killers) are considerably more common in fiction than in real life. In fact, although many serial killers in recent history have been described as psychopathic, most psychopaths are not killers. Indeed, the argument has been made that many so-called 'high-performing' individuals, such as politicians or heads of large companies, show psychopathic tendencies to a greater degree than do individuals in other positions. That these have predominately been men may say more about the difficulties of women getting into these positions for reasons of gender bias, rather than a reduced propensity for psychopathy. It is both amusing and alarming to think that we may rely upon psychopaths to run our major institutions. This is because a tendency to psychopathy covers a range of traits such as egocentricity, ruthlessness, and a propensity for dissimulation. Often this is coupled with a degree of superficial charm and charisma which makes the rest of society, or the organisation within which the individual operates, even more vulnerable to their machinations, which goes some way towards explaining how they get into these positions in the first place.

Before we become too judgemental or paranoid about the possibility that our institutions are riddled with psychopaths, we should spare a thought for the possibility that modern organisations actually encourage this personality profile. In the way we vote or allow commerce to run itself, many people tacitly accept that the character profiles described above, however unlikeable they may be on a personal level, are precisely what is required to run a country or a large competitive company. In recent years, this dilemma has been most publicly played out in finance: nobody likes to see rogue traders and fat-cats playing high-stakes games with national economies for huge personal gain, but the defence most commonly cited to curb further regulation of the banking system is that, essentially, we rely upon the same people to drive the engine of international finance. This is not an argument that everyone accepts. Nevertheless, historically speaking, and with only rare exceptions, society has defaulted towards the realpolitik of allowing individuals with these tendencies to do these jobs, even if it is inevitably coupled with the hazard of the collateral damage they often bring with them. Enoch Powell[39] resolved our collective cognitive dissonance by observing that at least these careers usually end in a sense of failure, allowing the rest of us to feel better about the thought that there is some natural justice in the end.

The argument appears famously in the film *A Few Good Men*, in which a central character – a marine general played by Jack Nicholson – presents the case that moral and legal arguments in individual cases of command should not apply to him because, as a commander on the front line of conflict, his type alone have the ability to do a job that others cannot do, or choose not to do. By this logic, society is therefore not in a position to make moral arguments about his behaviour: 'You want me on that wall; you NEED me on that wall'. In terms of the moral issue at hand in the story (the general illegally ordered an assault on one of his own men which led to his death), the film seeks to have it both ways by indicting the general in a court martial at the same time as encouraging the viewer to accept that the general has a valid, if uncomfortable, point.

In respect to Richard III, the same balance applies with the additional nuance that the tolerance to brutality in the 15th century was somewhat higher: Richard was undoubtedly responsible (or held responsible) for acts that shocked, or at least offended, the sensibilities of his contemporaries. But are we looking at the actions of a normal, high-performing individual in

---

39   Enoch Powell (1912–1998). A British scholar and Conservative MP whose own career as a cabinet minister declined after making inflammatory speeches about unlimited immigration.

a leadership position? Or are we looking at an individual whose behaviour is aberrant to the point of being called monstrous at the time? We can see that the boundary that separates reasonable brutality (for the 15th century) from monstrous behaviour (by 21st-century standards) is a fine judgement call. This chapter attempts to unpick the elements of psychopathy to look in greater detail to consider whether Richard matches what we would have expected of a psychopathic killer. We need to be clear about this: Richard was directly responsible for deaths such as those of Hastings or Buckingham. But both of these were seen as legitimate executions at the time. Other deaths are a matter of conjecture, although he seems, on balance of probability, also to have been responsible for the deaths of his two nephews. He may have shown tendencies to personality traits often associated with psychopathy, such as a degree of narcissism – indeed I argue below that it would be surprising if he did not. But the question is whether he took an *abnormal* satisfaction in cruelty and killing, and used it, by choice, to achieve goals where others would have found alternative means.

Before going into detail, there are three general reasons why it is unlikely that Richard was some form of monster. First, statistically speaking, and by modern definitions at least, psychopathic killers are extremely rare. In recent years in Britain, Dennis Nilson, Ian Brady and Myra Hindley, Peter Manuel, and the Wests come to mind. They represent a fraction of a percentage of prisoners currently in custody. True, death by suicide or judicial execution is more common for such people, but the fact remains that this is not a *likely* mental disorder, and we would seek substantial corroborative evidence to place such a diagnosis on Richard III. Second, even accounting for the brutality of the times, we should not think that medieval observers were unable to discriminate extreme mental conditions from more 'normal' behaviour. For example, Henry VI's mental frailty was apparent to all, as was Vlad the Impaler's (a near-contemporary of Richard) unusual pleasure in cruelty. In his case, records say it amused him to take beggars off the street for a meal in court to have them then burned alive for being a burden on his society. People could, and still can, tell the difference between the eccentric and the aberrant. Had Richard demonstrated such tendencies, we can have expected at least some contemporary commentary or hints to have emerged to that effect. There are none. Finally, we should remember that the events that damage Richard's reputation took place in the turbulence of his last three years as he managed the transition from Protector to King. Prior to that, disregarding a degree of aggression that would not be seen as particularly unusual for the times, his reputation was one of a loyal brother and a just and respected Head of the Council of the North. Serious psychopathology is generally evident very much earlier in life than that. The complete absence of evidence of psychopathic behaviour prior to the age of 30 – which his contemporaries could have been expected to spot – points away from this diagnosis.

This is not to say that Richard did not display some traits closely associated with psychopathy. Some psychologists characterise serious psychopathy in terms of a 'dark triad' of personality traits, giving special attention to two: narcissism and Machiavellianism, to be assessed alongside a third trait – as it happens, and confusingly, also termed as psychopathy. The distinction between these traits is blurred and we should not see them as absolutes. For descriptive purposes, however, they are a useful way of talking about the complexity of the issue.

Narcissus was a self-absorbed young man in Greek legend who fell in love with his own reflection in a pool and was punished by the gods by being transformed into a daffodil (hence the Latin name *narcissus* for that plant family). As a psychological concept, narcissistic personality disorder is seen as an excessive and grandiose self-regard, and an unregulated need for attention coupled with a corresponding lack of empathy for corresponding needs in everyone else. This can lead to excessive arrogance and aggression. In mild form, most children are inherently narcissistic and an important element of the socialisation of children is the process by which the child comes to consider the needs and entitlements of other people. Unsurprisingly, children with no siblings often fall into the 'only one' syndrome which has some of these characteristics. The issue, of course, is whether the child learns to moderate their drive to satisfy their own needs in order to function in society.

In practice, 'excessive' narcissism is not often defined on its own, or as a prognosis of worse to come. More likely, it is diagnosed *after the event* as a contributory element in a broader pattern of behaviour that can be described as psychopathic. The implication is that narcissistic personality disorder does not *necessarily* lead to psychopathically criminal behaviour, but in the event that such behaviour is observed, it is more likely that excessive narcissism is present as part of the personality profile. This is important because, from the onset, in the case of Richard III, a degree of arrogance and self-regarding is to be expected given his status. If anything, however, the evidence is counter-indicative. Taking his brothers Edward and George as useful comparators, neither of whom have been described as monsters, Richard appears less, rather than more, likely to be described that way. Edward IV led something of a hedonistic life and was reputed to have seduced women at knifepoint. George appears in hindsight to have been impulsive, fickle, greedy, and self-important. He also appears to have been responsible for questionable executions for which he had no authority in law. Richard, on the other hand, at least in York, adopted a leadership style that, from the accounts of the time, can be described as balanced insofar as it appears largely to have been with the approval of the consensus and includes occasions where he operated palpably for the common good rather than just in his own interest. This is *not* to say that Richard did not operate in his own interest. Horrox shows quite clearly that he did, and that he was ruthless in doing so. It also does not in itself absolutely exclude the possibility that Richard was a murderous narcissistic psychopath, but for the moment we simply observe that little or no substantive evidence of excessive narcissism per se appears in the historical record.

We now move on to the second of the so-called 'dark triad' traits. In Machiavelli's[40] *The Prince* (1513), his most famous work, he presents dishonesty and serious activities (such as killing individuals whose guilt is unproven) as the normal cut-and-thrust of politics, what we now call realpolitik. The logic of his argument is effectively to endorse this behaviour, although this may not have been his primary intention. As a result, describing someone as 'Machiavellian' is to describe them as deceitful and deviously manipulative, if not downright evil. In a model of effective criminal psychopathy, an individual motivated by strong narcissist tendencies uses Machiavellian (i.e. devious and oblique) methods to achieve their ends because any direct declaration of those aims would be both socially unacceptable and, being visible, more easily thwarted.

Immediately we see a number of characteristics associated with criminal psychopathy that emerge. First, effective deception requires well-developed cognitive skills. As Scott wrote: '*What a tangled web we weave, when first we practise to deceive!*' Deception on a large scale is a difficult business. Beyond an emotional capacity for bare-faced lying and an ability to ignore or override any sense of guilt, it requires planning, analysis, and a good memory. Detectives worldwide function by exploring the inconsistencies and inaccuracies of their prisoner's alibi, and have developed any number of techniques to stretch their suspect's memory and coherence of detail to breaking point. Most are not up to it and their story breaks down. The corollary of this is that, when a criminal psychopath has functioned for some time, when the deviousness of their behaviour is finally

---

40 Niccolo Machiavelli (1469–1527) lived and died in Florence as a near-contemporary of Richard and was a senior politician in the Florentine republic.

revealed, the common perception is of them having higher-than-average intellectual skills. To be a high-performing individual you need innate intelligence, and this applies to a high-performing psychopathic criminal as much as it does to a politician or a corporate head.

A second point to emerge is that if an individual is to use Machiavellian methods to operate, they usually need to be effective in interpersonal communication. This reveals two other common traits. First, psychopaths are often associated with a degree of charisma, and in some cases seem able to hold individuals in thrall, individuals who may even know the extent of their evil behaviour. The pairing of Ian Brady and Myra Hindley comes to mind. There is a common misunderstanding here. Psychopaths are often described as callous and cruel, lacking empathy for other human beings. Certainly in the case of murderous individuals, they are capable of being cruel, but it does not mean they do not understand emotion. On the contrary, it is more likely that they have an acute sense of other people's emotional needs and an ability to manipulate them accordingly. It is likely that in the worst cases, far from being unable to understand or even empathise with other people's feelings, the narcissist's perception that their needs take precedence over all others provides the contempt that allows them to be so deceitful and manipulative.

This brings us to what is meant by *psychopathy* as the third element of the Dark Triad. Essentially, it is no more than the judgement that the personalities' tendency to narcissism and Machiavellianism is both, in degree and in terms of the objectives to which they are applied, beyond what is normal. Richard may have had narcissistic tendencies, and he was clearly capable of dissembling and being devious in a Machiavellian way. However, examination of Richard's life is consistent with the view that this was not seen at the time as anything particularly out of the ordinary until his assumption of the throne. That – and the events contingent upon that – turned public opinion against him. This is much more to do with the growing conclusion in the country that Richard's actions were seen as crossing critical boundaries and does not need to include the hypothesis that Richard was, all along, a psychopath.

We can also look at different trajectories in psychopathic careers to see that Richard does not fit a usual pattern. Perhaps the most predictable element of psychopathy to be considered here is a strong element of narcissism, where the dominant psychological motivator is an unsocialised sense of self-importance. It follows from this that narcissists have a strong need to exert control in life (lest anyone else compromises their self-interest) and an accompanying alertness to threat verging upon paranoia. Where this exceptional drive is present, and depending upon the individual's social skills in early life, it will develop in two different ways. For some, perhaps those lacking in social skills or simple communicative skills at key developmental stages, it will lead them away from trying to control the people around them; because, for whatever reason, that does not achieve their ends. Instead they develop a modus operandi in which they can limit the effects of other people on *them* – they become outsiders obsessed with the privacy of their own thoughts and control of their own life. This may be accompanied by schizoid tendencies. Such a psychology is naturally primed towards antisocial attitudes and resentment. Self-isolating, and therefore filtering out any feedback that does something other than fuel this position, such individuals are potential time bombs whose behaviour can be triggered to violence. This argument has been used to explain a number of killing sprees, including: Hungerford; Utoya Island, Norway; Dunblane; Port Arthur, Tasmania; and Carlisle. It is probably the default explanation for all such mass murders. This is close to the model Shakespeare gives us of Richard – a devious, deeply resentful, and cunning man prepared to bide his time before waiting for the opportunity to strike.

However, examining Richard's first 30 years, this seems unlikely. Here, records of his demeanour do not emphasise deviousness, resentment, or social exclusion (although perhaps he was not as socially fluid as his brother Edward IV). Rather, he appears as reasonably professional: capable of forming useful working relationships. To describe him as *prima inter pares*[41] would be to go too far, because he most certainly would see himself of royal blood, subject only to the King. To propose that these 30 years reflect Richard's continued biding of time, alongside a well-developed ability to hide his intentions, is implausible. This is not to say, as Hicks and others have suggested, that dissimulation was not a significant aspect of his personality. The argument is whether what is known of him constitutes evidence for psychopathy. To maintain this image, a truly psychopathic Richard would have had to have been extraordinarily self-controlled over a sustained period of time – he was an influential character for some 15 years before Edward's death – during which any number of temptations to express his true nature would have presented themselves. In the absence of any evidence to suggest otherwise, there is no good reason to entertain this hypothesis.

For the more socially skilled, psychopathic narcissism has an alternative trajectory that we should also consider here. Far from being unable to empathise with other people's feelings, such individuals can be unusually adroit in understanding the other's needs. However, in their case, their general contempt for others feelings allows them greater licence in how they use this skill. This admixture of highly tuned social intelligence unfettered by moral constraint gives them a strong social advantage that allows some psychopaths to become very powerful people: it allows them to be highly charismatic, and at other times ruthless and controlling. This enables them to hold close associates in thrall and fear in equal measure.

---

41 'First among equals'.

Expressed in this way, narcissism can be associated with strong elements of controlling behaviour in asymmetric (by which we mean exclusively controlled on one side) interpersonal relationships. Such people, confident in their ability to control and taking pleasure in demonstrating it, may make compelling leaders, but they can also be very careless in their relationships and gratuitously cruel. Henry VIII seems a good example of this, although even here we must be cautious before labelling him as a psychopathic, since 16th-century kings – referred to for the first time as 'Your Majesty' as opposed to 'Your Grace' – were genuinely raised to see themselves as the most important person in everyone's lives. But this also does not appear to have been Richard's way, at least not in an extreme form. While Richard may have been no bon viveur, his reputation at York was of steadiness and a strict observance of justice for all – even against his own interests. We should not forget, however, that in this he may have been considering his longer-term interests and how he wished to be perceived.

These judgements cannot be absolute and clear-cut. Should one choose to be selective, there are many examples of Richard's behaviour around which one might construct quite a plausible case for psychopathy, or at least lead us to think more seriously in those terms: Hicks emphasises Richard's dissimulation and general deviousness; the pattern of his usurpation is not inconsistent with a worked-out plan[42]; his ability to persuade Vaughan and Grey not to resist his taking control of Edward V could be seen as evidence

---

42   The problem with this as any evidence for Richard's psychopathy is that he could not have anticipated the timing or the circumstances of Edward IV's death. So, whatever plan there was (apart from broad considerations), must have been improvised at the time: and in response to events as much as attempting to control them. It is not unreasonable to think that Richard considered the various possibilities and timings of Edward IV's death and had some strategy for an appropriate response. However, in his position, that would merely be prudent rather than representing some form of cunning plan.

of a charismatic and controlling character; and his vindictiveness towards them and Rivers is also characteristic of these tendencies. To this, of course, must be added the unexplained disappearance of the princes in the Tower, the responsibility for which most likely falls upon Richard and those following his instructions.

Does such a list point to Richard as a full-blown psychopath? Medieval monarchy was institutionally inclined to violence, and Richard was no exception to this. The facts of the various deaths around him, nor any other evidence, lend little support to the idea that he was inclined to violence or cruelty more than was necessary, or that he took unusual pleasure in this. He may well have shown personality characteristics that take him closer to tendencies we might describe as psychopathic, but this is of its times. If later propaganda picked up on some of these tendencies, this is not to be surprised at, and it should not change the conclusions. We also should not forget that modern research suggests that many people in senior positions of authority show the same profile. We can speculate that Richard may not have been a particularly easy person to like. He may also have been a difficult person to communicate with. Some of his actions, such as the execution of Hastings, may also have been hasty or may have lacked a steady moral compass, but there is no evidence here to suggest he had a serious personality disorder that would allow us to describe him as a psychopathic killer.

Chapter Nine

Retrospective

This final chapter revisits the objectives set at the beginning of the book, and the outstanding question of what, if anything, a psychological perspective of an historical figure delivers. Does a combination of approaches – *psychohistory*, if you like – have any intellectual validity? Or is it merely a contrived marriage? As proposed marriages go, it seems a plausible match. Psychological science is concerned with studying the relationship between motivation, knowledge, and behaviour. Historians and biographers will certainly agree that understanding these aspects of historical figures is central to their discipline too. Yet any synergy one might have expected between these disciplines on the basis of that common premise is scant. Indeed, if anything, relations have often been hostile. Consider the case of Dixon's *On the Psychology of Military Incompetence* (1976)[43], where, for example, a Freudian analysis is used to explain Douglas Haig's performance as leader of the British Expeditionary Force in France during World War I.

Of this, one biographer of Haig wrote:

---

43 *On the Psychology of Military Incompetence* N.F. Dixon (1976) Pimlico London, ISBN 0-7126-5889-0.

Dixon's work is the most dangerous because of the way in which apparently scientific approach is used. ... Blinded by 'psychology' the reader is apparently not supposed to notice backward and twisted reasoning ... The book tells us a great deal more about the psychology and indeed the incompetence of psychohistorians than that of military commanders.

(DeGroot, 1988)[44]

In fairness, many psychologists will have sympathised with this attitude. Although Dixon could subsequently argue that the purpose of his book was largely misunderstood by historians (but tellingly not by the military), the argument that Haig was an incompetent sadist came across as partial, incautious, and thereby self-defeating. It can also be said that, although relatively rare, good use of psychological argument in historical reasoning has come from historians themselves. An interesting example would be Keegan's *The Face of Battle* (1976)[45], which looks at the human experience at Agincourt, Waterloo, and the Somme.

But the argument cannot be left there, for two reasons. First, whilst DeGroot may have felt justified in his line towards Dixon, his words are pernicious and more general. Must the science of psychology *necessarily* blind us to historical insight from another perspective? Are all psychohistorians incompetent? And are all attempts at 'psychohistory' doomed to failure? I fear this reflects an established attitude. In earlier versions of publications related to this book I received comments from a number of different historians including:

Do the authors know anything about 15th century mental structures and habits of thought? ... There is a danger that this chapter will be full of speculation and cliché ... it is generally

---

44 *Douglas Haig, 1861–1928* G. DeGroot (1988) Unwin Hyman Ltd London, ISBN 0-04-440192-2.

45 *The Face of Battle* J. Keegan (1976) Jonathan Cape London, ISBN 0-224-01232-0.

accepted that you cannot psycho-analyse the dead. I suspect it
will be popular with Ricardians and a tremendous pain to the
rest of us.

Not all unreasonable, perhaps; and readers of this book must draw their own conclusions. But one senses disciplinary ownership, exclusivity, and even an intention to sting, as P.G. Wodehouse's Bertie Wooster would have put it. For some reason, there was a presumption that the book would be biased towards a pro-Ricardian line. Perhaps historians of Richard III are used to opposition from Ricardians and, by a form of negative attribution, assumed that another approach, equally disapproved by professional historians, must come from the same direction. Worse, the remarks are based upon a clichéd ignorance as to what psychologists have got to say. Psychoanalysis, for example, is rarely taught in British psychology schools and barely figured in this book at all. Here, one of the aims has been to justify and illustrate some psychological approaches historians and others may not have seen applied in this context before and which they may find useful. I leave it to others to judge whether, thus informed and from their own perspective, such approaches add value to the interpretation of history, if only by looking at issues from a new perspective. Hardly synergy, perhaps, but some first steps to a more constructive relationship.

One of the genuine concerns that would be shared by historians and psychologists alike is to worry that a contemporary analysis always risks distorting the psychology of 15th-century people. L.P. Hartley's opening sentence to the novel *The Go-Between* (1953), '*The past is a foreign country: they do things differently there*', may now seem a little over-used, but it speaks to this issue. We are interested if, and how, contemporary approaches to psychology can inform historical analysis or whether the circumstances are so different that our contemporary knowledge and psychological understanding is simply inappropriate. Insofar as it is possible, this book has sought to present those psychological motivations, and the mechanisms they represent, that are common to all humans. For example, I argue that the way in which the human mind perceives and analyses the decisions it has to make is the product of an evolutionary process. This has, by and large, finessed the problem of how a limited (if highly complex) biological structure such as the brain manages the overwhelming mass of information it needs to process to stay alive. To any particular human, much of the information it receives is not relevant (while some of it could become so very soon); and of the rest, some key elements may be missing or obscured. As developers of artificial intelligence discovered some time ago, the real world does not readily submit to analysis that reveals a single and unambiguous interpretation and which points to an equally unambiguous course of action. What we actually do is a form of analysis in which the mind gambles on the basis of informed guesses. Many of these psychological processes (although there was not space in the book to do full justice to the matter) are biased in some way or another towards models we already have of the world in our mind. This is in the sense that, by and large, we see the world as we expect it to be, and this bias serves a wider evolutionary purpose of preserving the individual, or at least the species, in the long run. All of our perceptions of the world are distorted and interpreted in these terms. This characteristic of the human mind applied as much in the 15th century as it does in the present.

To digress for a moment, it is not hard to see that the fractious debate between psychology and history is itself fuelled by this state of affairs. One effect of this basic human property has been that expertise has become tribal, and intellectuals spanning more than one field (so-called polymaths) are now seen rarely, if at all. Practitioners in a particular discipline are trained and placed at one remove, both from laymen, and from experts in another field. Thus, for example, to deal with human subjectivity and the limitations of human memory, and at the same time to generate tools to investigate the natural world, mathematicians have developed a massive edifice of abstract notations, theorems, and proofs, all of which have to be mastered even to reach a basic competence in mathematics. Similarly, historians agree on, and vigorously defend, their analytical techniques and materials. And to be competent in any particular field of history, they learn as much as they can – in breadth and depth – about that area as background context. Psychologists likewise develop their own experimental methods and theoretical approaches.

Such expertise is possible because the human mind assimilates knowledge in terms of what it has already learned. In one sense this is a virtuous circle: the more you know, the more you can learn. But in another sense, it is a divisive circle: the effect of these specialisations is not only to make expertise less accessible to the layman, but it also places boundaries between academic disciplines. In today's world, the expert in psychology is the layman in history. Naturally, these boundaries are defended, as in the heated debate over psychohistory, because domain experts can quite reasonably claim that they best know how their discipline should conduct itself. But this is as much a political act as it is an intellectual judgement because evaluations of intellectual worth are made largely by those people most invested in the status quo: the leaders in that academic discipline. Ultimately, in the nature of university governance, these evaluations are worth money, power, and influence, and these are powerful motivators in human society[46]. This is arguably why some fashions in psychological research have persisted rather longer than their scientific merit alone would suggest, and it is also a justification for why unorthodox approaches should be encouraged rather than vilified or ignored. Expertise and creativity are not always natural bedfellows.

---

46 And so Juneval's famous question of how to hold powerful people to account: '*Quis custodiet ipsos custodies?*' – *Who watches the watchmen?* – applies as much to academic life as it does to any other human endeavour.

Returning to the application of modern psychology to 15th-century figures, this book concentrates upon aspects of psychology such as: decision-making, personality theory, developmental psychology, and social psychology that we can reasonably expect, with some sensitivity to the context of the times, to apply to Richard III and his society. I have taken some trouble to establish that the human mind in key respects is unchanged from the 15th century. It neither has had time to evolve biologically nor to become so remote socially for them not to be relevant. And yet we need to remember that the world was indeed very different. For example, the existence of heaven and hell was believed absolutely, with obvious consequences for the immortal soul. Furthermore, the world was understood to have been created by God: all human things were ordered in a great chain of being in which kings, and then noblemen, were deemed superior to the peasantry, and men were considered superior to women. Social strata were thereby fixed and social mobility practically impossible. The concepts of place in society, duty to one's betters, and the observance of religious devotion are therefore much more potent than today. Conversely, concepts of free will, religious tolerance, and a premium placed upon creative thinking – prized in the modern world – would be seen as subversive and heretical, and risked sanction.

The constraints of this context are central to interpreting the formulation of Richard's personality here. For example, on reflection, it is really not much of a revelation to suggest that, in the Big Five elements of personality, Richard probably registered as 'less than average' with respect to 'openness to new experience', at least in relation to what we in the 21st century would expect. According to scholars, Richard, as King, behaved and disposed his court and governance much as his predecessors did. He was not particularly innovative. He was also authoritarian and fixed in his views about justice and religion. But to do or be anything else is to expect rather a lot. At this time, it was believed that all knowledge (or at least that knowledge the Catholic Church was allowing, given that some classical writings were proscribed) was to be found in the Bible and the writings of the approved ancient philosophers. At this time, scientific and technical developments were proceeding at a very slow pace, although a scientific renaissance was beginning. For example, Copernicus was developing a new view of the heavens in which the earth was not central to the universe but going around the sun. This was highly controversial. Nearly one hundred years later Galileo narrowly avoided being burned at the stake for endorsing similar views. For that reason, Copernicus himself went to some trouble to suggest that his system was merely a convenience of calculation rather than a statement of scientific fact. For a man in Richard's position, social and intellectual innovation was unsafe, and in any case unlikely, because there was no motivation for it.

Many historians have already come to similar conclusions about Richard's character to those drawn here. What then, is new about this analysis? I argue that a psychological perspective adds value in two respects. Firstly, it provides a plausible, and moreover coherent, view of Richard over his entire lifetime. This is based upon a commonly understood thread of psychological theory based upon his earliest years. This offers us an authoritarian, resilient, and acquisitive personality, prone sometimes to vindictiveness, and prone also to an intolerance of uncertainty that could even lead sometimes to impulsive or aggressive acts. This arises in part from a genetic inheritance, a schooling in dynastic duties, and a younger child's need to develop coping strategies as the youngest and weakest of a sibling cohort. From this point of view, Richard's personality is of a piece. Secondly, there is every reason to believe that these psychological dynamics, very familiar in the 21st century, were also in recognisable in the 15th century. By reference to the same personality traits we can observe around us today, we therefore have some insight into the complexity and individuality of this long-dead human being.

There is a seeming contradiction in this that can usefully be expanded here. On the one hand, the argument is being made that many very different personalities exhibit the traits associated with Richard. Richard could be like any of these people or different to them all. On the other hand, I have argued that this gives us more insight into Richard as an individual. How can I make this claim? What I have sought to do – consistent with the first objective of this book being to establish a common cause between psychology and historical analysis – is to reconnect us with Richard as a human being rather than a character in an historical narrative. We are exploring the point that, while Richard was a king having to make some extraordinary decisions (in the sense that most of us are not called upon to make similarly momentous choices), he did so with psychological mechanisms that can be described as entirely familiar to psychologists and indeed to us all. We are being invited to understand Richard in terms we understand about ourselves and people we know, at the same time being offered some sense of how variable the expression of those mechanisms can be in a given individual.

A second objective of this book was to take the opportunity to dispel some misconceptions of how psychology might be applied in this context and, in so doing, offer a different perspective of the discipline that is interesting and useful. These misconceptions are rooted in a problem of disciplinary ownership that both historians and psychologists share: they are both fields that, at a superficial level, are readily available to the layperson. We can assimilate self-knowledge about behaviour, motivation, and beliefs, just as we can learn about history from watching television, but in neither case does it makes us experts. Similarly, a problem psychologists experience in representing their expertise is that – based upon an intuitive sense of self-knowledge – everyone feels entitled to make psychological arguments. However, what a psychological training delivers is an understanding of just how misleading intuition can be, and how important it is to recognise how the behaviour and reasoning of an ordinary person operates in extraordinary circumstances. Otherwise, this might lead us to think that people who achieve extraordinary things have extraordinary powers or 'gifts', or that everyone associated with a heinous crime is necessarily a psychopath. Either or both may be true, but not necessarily so. The gap between lay understanding and psychological expertise is wider than people think and poorly understood.

To extend the argument, for psychologists, some of the more interesting insights emerge when explanations for behaviour are counterintuitive to our everyday understanding, or are hidden; only emerging when we adopt perspectives not previously considered. I use an example of this from my own research: the design of new computerised systems can, paradoxically, be based upon an appropriate understanding of why paper-based systems become so untidy, and how people actually *use* them. There is something useful to learn about why certain kinds of untidy offices are, in fact, highly functional in a way that tidy offices could not be. To broaden the issue, this is also a defence of Dixon's *On the Psychology of Military Incompetence*: however bizarre and socially unacceptable a psychological hypothesis might be to the public at large, it can represent an informed, coherent attempt to make specific points. The dismissal of a psychologist's arguments as 'psycho-babble' (or perhaps more carefully put as 'clichéd and speculative') is therefore unreasonable if it reflects a lack of understanding of the scientific argument being made or the intended status of the hypotheses being entertained. Dixon's aim was to provoke readers into thinking differently about the qualities of military leadership, and in this he most certainly succeeded.

Historians take a similar issue with 'popular history' and quite reasonably defend the concept of a trained historian. As I understand it, immersion in historical sources and a broad understanding of their historical context and provenance are key: hence the comment in the anonymous review quoted earlier in this chapter above about understanding how people thought in the 15th century.[47] They will also argue that understanding the historical context – the historian's stock-in-trade – is all, and that applying modern psychological approaches is inappropriate. Their argument, in short, is that people thought differently in the past because their world was indeed different, and assessing historical figures by the benchmarks of the present is misleading.

In fact, psychological research readily supports the premise but not the conclusion that flows from it. The notion of *situated cognition* – that our very thoughts and beliefs are integrally structured and constrained by our context – has been recently re-energised by the IT revolution and the notion that the technology we use, and the way we think while using it, are integrally linked. There is substance to the concern that the mobile phones we now routinely use and rely upon, are materially affecting the way we think, the way we plan our actions, and the way we operate in society. That idea has direct resonance, of course, in archaeological research relating the evolution of human cognition to the development of artefacts. Other psychological research points to broader cultural factors that influence our manner of thought. As observed earlier, Nisbett[48], for example, argues that the whole framework of thinking in the Western world differs from that in the East because of the underlying philosophies embedded in their culture. The West is underpinned by Greek philosophy, which emphasises the atomistic relationships between individual entities in terms of the actions and reactions upon them. On the other hand, the philosophy of Confucious in the East is more concerned with the complex flow of fields of entities. Thought and behaviour

---

47   Although it is hard to return to this review without asking whether historians or psychologists should feel equally confident about understanding mental structures and habits of thought, 15th century or otherwise.

48   R.E. Nisbett is a contemporary American psychologist interested in culture and systems of thought. For example, see Nisbett, Peng, Choi, and Norenzayan, *Psychological Review* 108 (2001) pp 291–310.

is indeed strongly influenced by the material and intellectual context of the times. Clearly it is important to understand the context in which we are observing human behaviour and decision-making.

Nevertheless, this argument cannot in itself be used to invalidate a psychological analysis of historical figures. If it did, all human behaviour being in context, it would render any form of scientific generalisation impossible. The progress of psychology over the past 100 years suggests otherwise. It does mean, however, that psychologists should enter this arena with caution. In the case of Richard III, this is particularly so. Over 500 years have elapsed, and the world manifestly is a very different place with different social structures and different belief structures to go with them. Also, psychology is an empirical science, and making strong claims about personality often requires hours of interview and the application of psychometric techniques, none of which is available here. Indeed, probably because of some selective culling of information by the Tudors, the documentary evidence of Richard's monarchy is thin, and further, much of what survives has to be viewed through the lens of Tudor propaganda. We have to recognise that with such scant information, any conclusions we offer are speculative, however informed, and that we risk these speculations being taken up in a highly polarised historical debate. This was never a low-risk intellectual exercise.

However, there are good reasons to take such risks, not in the least being that stretching the boundaries of established disciplines is probably worthwhile its own right. The current interest in Richard III creates the opportunity for psychology to show its worth to a wider audience. In the spirit of 'proof of concept', we can call for psychological approaches to history to be judged in their own right, and specifically not to be adjudicated by historians alone. Historians might be concerned about psychologists' theorising about historical figures. But equally, they are not averse to making such psychological assertions themselves, and quite rightly: the whole point of their exercise is to construct a coherent narrative and understanding of historical figures and events. But just as an historian's well-tuned sense of their historical period permits such speculation, is it not equally true that psychologists' experience of behaviour in context gives the same permission? And furthermore, being based upon different premises derived from psychological theory, is it not equally valid to argue that this perspective is deserving of hearing in its own right?

Thus the second purpose of this book was to present psychology to a wider audience. Psychology is one of those subjects that both attract a great deal of interest, as evidenced by the wide range of popular magazines available, and, when it suits, a fair degree of derision when it can be accused (fairly or not) of losing contact with the real world. That Sigmund Freud is commonly seen as the stereotypical psychologist is no help either. It may be that a reappraisal of Freud's work is overdue – I happen to believe that it is – but the caricature of psychology inherited from Freud is a gross distortion of what most psychologists actually do. As a result, when talking to laypersons, psychologists often feel driven to a form of mental gymnastics where the main aim is to avoid feeding and encouraging common beliefs about psychology we may not intend, while at the same time saying something meaningful and interesting. This is certainly difficult, but no excuse for not trying.

As a means to this end, this book brings together a range of psychological ideas within the evolutionary theories of Charles Darwin. In the evolutionary approach to understanding the mind, we are constantly mindful that we are studying an entity 'permanently under reconstruction': the way we think and behave is a product of ongoing evolutionary pressures. In the psychological theory discussed, what I have sought to illustrate is how the mind and personality are the product of this. As I have argued throughout this book, the world is a very 'noisy' place where one of the main pressures on our ability to think effectively is to divine what is important in the world around us and what is not. Very severe demands of information processing have to be managed by biological systems which are very simple in themselves, but which have had time to evolve in rather complex ways. The product is a system in which the mind not only processes complex information but operates as part of a social structure that enables the human community to become stronger and more resilient than the sum of its parts.

Nature's solution is a mind that makes informed assumptions about the world. We use our prior knowledge, honed in childhood, to minimise the processing we do by filling the predictable gaps. What we often think of as thinking and analysing is actually memory of known patterns and, when necessary, a refiguring of our model of reality to make these pieces fit. We are rarely aware of this, but the other side of this coin is that what we experience as our existence and our understanding of the outside world is neither coherent nor complete. But it is usually sufficient for our needs. Furthermore, the system has with it a set of checks and balances – themselves acutely tuned to the way the world is – to enable us to adjust when that sufficiency breaks down.

What is fascinating in this is the gap between our intuitive experience of how these processes work and what is actually taking place. The study of psychology is therefore replete with counterintuitivity and misunderstanding. For example, a sudoku expert might describe what they do as analysis. For the most part it is not: they are recalling facts and procedures that deliver results from memory. Likewise, chess experts do not necessarily think 'better' or 'quicker': they simply know more and are more practised in their domain of expertise. When we curse other people for being bad drivers, we are making a simple guess. It does not occur to us that they might be perfectly good drivers and the situation is not quite as it seems. These are everyday perceptions of human thought, appearing to be one thing, but often, actually, being something different.

A key element of this is that in so many cases, human behaviour that appears extraordinary is in fact the application of absolutely commonplace cognitive processing applied to an unusual circumstance. Notions that an individual is 'gifted' or 'psychopathic' or has 'photographic memory' all confer upon the individual some quasi-mystical quality, something extra, that 'explains' their behaviour, be it terrible or quite exceptional in other ways. But time and time again, psychologists have been able to show that exceptional behaviour is entirely explainable in terms of ordinary processes expressed in unusual circumstances[49]. The pianist who can remember a concerto not played for two years just knows more about piano concertos and probably how to reconstruct them if necessary. The memory expert who can recall hundreds of objects or numbers in the correct order is using strategies that you and I would not have thought of by ourselves. But if we are taught these methods, we can emulate their performance. I hope that, by contextualising some of these issues in terms of seeking an understanding of Richard of Gloucester, later King Richard III, I have been able to communicate something of the real nature of psychological science.

And what, in the final analysis, of the third objective: to seek a coherent understanding of Richard's humanity? This book was, after all, a search for some insight into what kind of person Richard might have been. I have painted a picture of someone whose piety, attention to detail, and focussed self-interest points to an authoritarian, controlling person. Whilst not pathological in the sense that he would have been seen as mad, I have argued that these would have been seen as defining characteristics of his personality, even in a 15th-century context. I have speculated further that these attributes, possibly exaggerated with what would otherwise been seen as inconsequential effects of his

---

49   The exception being those conditions which represent organic disorder of the brain, where my arguments clearly do not apply.

now-proven scoliosis, served him reasonably well as the King's brother, but less so in the crisis of 1483 as he became Protector and King. Before Edward IV's death, his efforts were largely aimed at constructing a Northern powerbase and only rarely did the King feel the need to instruct or admonish his brother, although his occasional acts of ruthlessness would have been evident to him. He was constructed, in public at least, as a dutiful brother, right-hand man to the King.

On the King's death, Richard felt driven to act. This analysis of his state of mind leads to the conclusion that he felt he could justify his assumption of the Crown both to himself and to the people at large, and that he came to this at a relatively early stage in the proceedings. In hindsight we can question whether this was a wise decision, but we can understand why an individual, feeling threatened and anxious to seek closure, while at the same time set on his own destiny, should make it. His ruthless effectiveness saw him through the process before society could react, but this was not the end of the story. Particularly after the rebellion of 1483, and for the remainder of his reign, there is a sense of siege. In this, his resilience and ability to function comes at a cost as we see his mounting political misfortunes mirrored in the concentric defences of his mind: as the going got tougher, those aspects of his personality that made him unpopular became more and more apparent.

This narrowing of behavioural repertoire and a reduced pragmatism is characteristic of a fixed mind under chronic stress. The more that stress built up, the harder he applied his well-worn strategies: he tried harder to be a 'good king'; he punished treason harder; and he subjected his opponents to greater and greater vilification. Horrox adds the speculation that he even sought self-redemption harder. It is a common saying that we can all try too hard and in so doing betray our weakness. We have all seen this characteristic both in ourselves and in others, and it is by those means that I attempt to illustrate Richard's humanity. Nevertheless, this pattern of behaviour could only further marginalise an individual whose social standing was already on the wane, as it was by September 1483. It would seem that, by then, a substantial portion of the Yorkist establishment neither believed his grounds for usurpation nor anything other than that he had murdered his nephews. How much this represented an accelerating movement, or a supposition of groupthink in hindsight, is hard to say, but erstwhile supporters like Stanley and Percy would have been aware of Richard's problem and would themselves have had views on the circumstances under which their loyalty would come to an end. This is not comparable to the last days of Hitler: defeat at Bosworth was far from inevitable and victory might have seen Richard consolidate. He was certainly neither mad nor sociopathic – and he clearly had close friends, but this was an increasingly closed circle that appeared to have been unable to help reverse the tide of Richard's unpopularity. If that analysis is correct, Richard's luck ran out at Bosworth. But if not then, his nemesis may not have been delayed long. By personality and by circumstance, Richard was unable to adapt, psychologically speaking, his modus operandi. The characteristics that propelled Richard into Kingship betrayed him in the aftermath, and Henry Tudor was the beneficiary.

Appendix One

Reductive approaches to personality theory and a few cautions

Apart from the sheer complexity of the subject matter (exactly how and why human beings differ from one another), most academic psychologists are very careful about the rigour of science in this area. Given the additional problems of applying psychological theory to historical figures, it is worth expanding on this to allow readers to judge the validity of my conclusions for themselves.

Caution is needed for at least three different reasons. First, we need to be confident of the technical competence of these theories: are the claims reasonable? Not all scientific 'discoveries' in this area in the past are now defendable. For example, in the 19th century the pseudo-science of phrenology led to the belief that elements of personality were linked to specific brain structures whose prominence could be inferred from the lumps and bumps on our skulls. This is now only remembered ornamentally by porcelain heads labelled with personality traits. That specific approach has been thoroughly debunked, and it reminds us that not every claim about new research proclaimed in the media or published in academic journals will actually pass the test of time.

A second caution is that personality theory, as in theories of intelligence, is based only upon data we choose to collect to study it. This circular argument leads to the famous put-down that intelligence is defined by the ability to perform well in intelligence tests. In the 19th century, one of the pioneers of this work, Francis Galton[50], thought that intelligence could be defined and measured more rigorously by speed of nerve conduction alone, and took simple physical reaction times as a basic measure of that. The argument essentially rested on the idea that if one individual's nervous system functioned quicker than another's, then it is to be expected that it would in all other respects be more efficient, leading to a biologically based and defendable definition of 'intelligence'. One may question the logic of that approach now, but the 19th century was a time of measurement for its own sake as much as theory-driven research. Researchers were looking for, and then exploring, phenomena in the real world. The tests that are used today are more complex and wide-ranging, but this still doesn't solve our basic problem: if anything, it makes it worse. Tests using verbal reasoning, arithmetic, or visual problems such as 'spot the difference' are sensitive to how much training the candidate has received. In this way, they are not 'pure' tests of intelligence because they have learnable components and possibly cultural elements too. George Bernard Shaw spells out the dangers of making judgements in such a way in his play *Pygmalion*, in which a working-class girl is trained to behave like a Lady and thereby pass as 'quality'. Thus, to extend the argument, if tests of personality are somehow polluted by culture, how can we theorise about personality without being influenced by present-day culture? And, given that most of this research is embedded in that of the past 60 years or so, how can we be sure that these theories will apply to individuals embedded in the culture of the 15th century? We have, at the very least, to be aware of the problem.

---

50 Francis Galton (1822–1911). A British polymath scientist and half-cousin of Darwin whose interest covered intelligence, statistics, sociology, and eugenics.

Our third caution is that not only is this reductive approach to human nature circular and culture-bound; it risks setting impossible demands upon science if the properties of complex systems are not always predictable from the understanding of their constituent parts. For scientists, this philosophical question goes to the very heart of what they do. Just because we want to believe that complex systems can be reduced to the sum of their parts, it doesn't actually mean that they can. This strategy of *reductionism* has worked well for science so far, but that doesn't necessarily guarantee anything either. After all, in some parts of the world, people bang pots and pans at the time of solar eclipses to drive the sun-swallowing dragon away. That has worked well for them so far, too. For an example of the problem of reductionism, it is said that the smell of ammonia cannot be predicted from what we know of its constituent elements, hydrogen and nitrogen. The smell might be an *emergent* property of the more complex whole that is an ammonia molecule. If it is truly an emergent property (and this question would go away with a new theory of the human olfactory system that can explain why ammonia smells the way it does), then it is not describable in reductionist terms. In summary, and returning to human personality, it may be that some attempts to explain personality in terms of combinations and balances of fundamental traits alone is just not possible.

Appendix Two

How far back can we go?

The process of evolution, in which living creatures (and indeed organisations and technology) adapt to changing circumstances means that, in applying modern psychology, we need to be sure that what we currently understand about the human mind, which for the most part is based upon the study of late-20th-century people, applies to people in the past. In this study of Richard III, does our modern understanding apply to someone who died over 500 years ago, or has the way the human mind works changed so much over the time elapsed as to make this impossible? Some historians get heated on this topic. To be clear, there are several issues in play. For one thing, we will have to ask how changes in society, culture, and its technological basis – all of which have certainly evolved over the past 500 years – have influenced behaviour. However, before that, we also need first to establish whether human beings, *as genetically determined biological entities*, have evolved in any significant way. Not only has the context changed, but it is possible that the nature of what it means to be a human being might also have changed. This prior question has to be resolved first before we make any claims about different modes of thinking in the 15th century as opposed to the present, and this is the aim of this appendix.

Beyond unearthing artefacts and sites, paleo-archaeologists have also studied the evolution of the human brain and how it has changed over time. This research comes to the conclusion that, in the analysis of historical figures, none is ancient enough to justify concern that the human brain has evolved to the point that it was comparably different from the present day. In Richard's case, 500 years is not significantly long enough to raise any concern whatsoever that, in biological terms, his *brain* was in any way less evolved or fundamentally different from our own. Indeed, so sure can we be of this that the same claim can equally be applied to the ancient classical culture some 1,400 years earlier.

How can we be so sure? One problem with studying how the human brain has evolved over time is that brain tissue does not survive fossilisation. This leaves brain volume, and the possibility of inferring brain structure from the interior of fossil skulls, as a crude measure of intellectual development to match against what can be inferred about behaviour from recovered artefacts such as tools or decorative items. On this basis, it seems that the greater brain capacity of early humans, in comparison to our nearest primate relatives, was first seen some 6 million years ago, but it only developed at a slow rate. At about 2 million years ago, our ancestors spread across the globe and their exposure to more widely varying climate types seems to have been associated with more rapid brain growth until about as recently as 200,000 years ago. Presumably, faced with the challenges of more difficult and less predictable climates, larger brains conferred an advantage which helped survival. Brain size reached a maximum with Neanderthal man, whose first appearance is dated at about 600,000 years ago. They are commonly believed to have become extinct about 40,000 years ago, although some argue that modern man (homo sapiens) shows some genetic record that can be attributed to cross-breeding with Neanderthals.

It is surprising to discover that brain size has *decreased* since Neanderthal man by some 10%, having previously tripled in size over the previous 2 million years. This is probably to say no more than size isn't everything. For one thing, although it represents about 2% of body mass, our brain's energy demands are disproportionate, at about 20% of the total. There is therefore an evolutionary pressure against brain *growth* per se, since it would also need to be accompanied with changes in metabolism and much larger hearts. Also, larger brains would need to develop after birth, as human brains do, and this would increase the dependency period of young children and decrease their chances of survival. More likely, noting that we, homo sapiens, out-evolved Neanderthals, the real evolutionary pressure is for selecting more efficient architecture and wiring of the brain. Such a conclusion is also consistent with studies of contemporary humans; these reliably show that, by any usual measure, brain size per se is not correlated to an individual's IQ or other measure of cognitive competence.

The implication is that most significant evolutions in human brain architecture took place hundreds of thousands of years ago. Some evidence has emerged to show that some human evolutions, such as the appearance of blue eyes and blond hair, are much more recent at about 10,000 years ago, and this reminds us that it would be wrong to forget that the process of evolution has not stopped. However, significant and successful mutations are rare, and occur in single cases which then propagate gradually across the population in subsequent generations. This would suggest that, with only some 550 years and about 25 generations having passed since Richard was born, it is highly unlikely that human brain anatomy is detectably different from the present, not least because in such a complex organism, significant changes probably require the conjunction of several mutations to have a significant effect. There are, however, some arguments that suggest that the rate of evolution is quickening or that significant evolutionary events can occur very quickly[51]. For one thing, the rate of evolution is influenced by the growth in population (because there are more births that increase the likelihood of a successful mutation being inserted into the gene pool). Also, greater prosperity and technological achievement has allowed culture to diversify more quickly. In effect, this increases the likelihood that genetic mutations will find a successful niche in the gene pool. However, even taking all of this into consideration, it still seems unlikely that either of these trends are sufficient to prevent us from making the claim that much of contemporary psychology can be applied to Richard III, provided we show due sensitivity to the cultural context of the 15th century.

---

51 At the beginning of the 19th century, the balance of two specific moths in the UK, one black and one white, was roughly 9:1 in favour of the white moth. By the end of the century, this ratio was almost exactly reversed for the simple reason that we had so blackened our environment with soot that the white moths were horribly conspicuous wherever they settled and were easily picked off by predators. In normal evolutionary terms, this particular change is lightning-fast. However, this emphasises the capacity of our technology to accelerate the processes of evolution. Given that we now have the ability to create extinction events such as a nuclear winter, this capacity is undeniable. However, here, we are looking into the past, and any claim that technological changes to date have instigated significant human evolution seems implausible.

ACKNOWLEDGEMENTS AND BACKGROUND

An interest in Richard III led to this book in two steps, linked in the person of Philippa Langley. First, she was the force behind the archaeological dig that excavated Richard III's burial site in the summer of 2012. Some archaeologists declared this to be a fool's errand and others entertained no high hopes at best. It takes a person of her drive to have made it happen at all. As we now know, certainly for the team on the ground and probably the rest of us, it exceeded expectations. In the second step, and with a healthy disregard for academic reserve, Philippa came to the School of Psychology at the University of Leicester to ask whether we would be able to contribute by developing a psychological profile of Richard. Rather like the dig, I doubt that many university colleagues had high expectations of such a maverick undertaking. Certainly a significant number of colleagues within the school were strongly opposed to it: they feared that the lack of available and reliable evidence compromised the scientific integrity of our discipline. For others outside psychology, attitudes varied from mild interest or benign indifference to sarcastic hostility. For myself, I had no doubt that this was an interesting thing to attempt, but I doubt that it would have happened had Philippa not pressed for it.

I am indebted to many other people without whom this book would never have been completed. Covering such a wide range of psychological expertise, it was enormously helpful to be able to call upon the expertise of colleagues and friends for their help and advice. Julian Boon and I co-authored a joint article on some of this material for *The Ricardian* in 2013. He was particularly helpful in material relating to the contents of Chapter Eight. I took pleasure, and learned a great deal, from conversations with Clive Hollin and Noelle Robertson. It goes without saying that any remaining errors or omissions in this book are mine and mine alone. Jim Horne, Rachael Ormerod, and Tom Ormerod were very generous with their time, and encouraging just at the point where I wondered whether the book would ever be published. All three saw through the flaws of earlier drafts to offer suggestions that improved the book immeasurably. Finally, but most importantly, I have to thank my partner Susan Lansdale. She not only engaged with the book through its long journey – improving it enormously in the process – but endured years of writer's angst. In this, she remained supportive throughout, at the same time as shrewdly guiding me away from a writer's self-indulgence. There are no words to express my thanks and admiration.

As a project, this book was fraught with risks and difficulties. Its parents are the disciplines of psychology and history, but it risked being disowned by both. If the past is anything to go by, each discipline is suspicious of multidisciplinarity, seeing it as a flawed chimera against the benchmarks of its self-defined norms. Life can be tough for such an orphan when it comes to publication. In this, the sheer scale of material to be covered in two domains of expertise, and the compromises necessary to bring them together, all increase the likelihood that either or both disciplines will find something to complain about. Additionally I set myself the goal of writing this primarily for the layperson for general interest: I hope the reader will find it an interesting story with relevance to themselves and the world they live in.

If, additionally, some scholars see it as a demonstration of the opportunities of multidisciplinarity, so much the better.

These risks and difficulties defined the way in which this book was presented, and I add a few notes here as background. The dilemma is how to communicate important ideas clearly that are complex and sometimes controversial. In the ideal, an accessibly plain English account, will encompass a psychological profile of Richard III and incorporate interesting and sometimes counter-intuitive ideas about how the human mind works. At the same time, for scientific integrity, it must avoid overstating the significance of particular theories whilst communicating the uncertainties and equivocations of the scientific debate.

My approach in this book is therefore to seek clear statements of psychological theory, largely free of qualifications and equivocations, in the belief in the reader's ability to judge for themselves what it is worth. I have minimised footnotes and external references throughout, although there are some. Where issues remain, or where some methodological digression is called for, I have taken it out of the main body of the text and consigned it to appendices. Similarly, the bibliography is not particularly long and is more in the spirit of further reading for those who want it.

The structure of the book follows the chronology of Richard's life closely because this makes obvious sense when considering the development of Richard's character. The chapters are mostly divided up by key stages of his life coupled with a discussion of psychological theory relevant to that stage of development. Although his reputation is mostly determined by his actions in the last two years of his life, the development of his personality must be tracked from before birth. It is not, however, an original biography: no new historical research has gone into this chronology. It is principally there to provide the essentials of Richard's life (especially for those not already familiar with it) as a framework upon which a psychological profile can be constructed. Consequently, the bibliography is largely of secondary texts and the chronology does not dwell on fine details of historical debate.

The agreed narrative of Richard's life that is used to construct a psychological profile here is not particularly controversial, although it is, of course, always possible that new documentary evidence could emerge in the future, or may lie, unrealised, in the minutiae of existing documents.

By chance, this book was planned and written in a time of political turmoil in Britain. I was struck by how much of the profile I was developing in Richard could be seen in contemporary leaders. But this is *not* to suggest an exact replication of Richard III is to be found in the present cohort. Elements of the profile I construct for Richard are evident in any number of them. But they are all different, even if they do share certain common traits. In drawing these parallels, therefore, I am attempting to enrich our understanding of Richard in two ways. First, I seek to flesh out some sense of his humanity, that he was a real man. Second, I draw attention to the different ways in which these traits express themselves in individuals. This is my way of having a cake and eating it. I have tried to give some insights into Richard III as a human being, but at the same time, I am attempting to communicate the uncertainties inherent in the undertaking.

For an academic psychologist I believe that scholarship becomes self-serving and introverted if it is not applied to new ventures which force us to explore our boundaries and question our conventions. If we do not take such risks we lack ambition and achieve less. But risks come with the possibility of failure. Optimists would say that such failure is the price of success elsewhere, to which I would add that it is nowhere near as expensive or depressing as the failure to take risks at all. On reading this book, I hope that you felt the risk worth taking. If not, then I hope you will forgive the attempt.

Mark Lansdale

Bibliography and further reading

Sources I have referred to directly are listed here, as are a number of books as background for further reading that might be interesting. In the case of the historical facts surrounding Richard III, since this book never sought to undertake ground-breaking historical research, I have only included sufficient additional references to enable the interested reader to pursue details and assess the broad consensus of the historical narrative. Similarly, the psychology texts I offer have been chosen to represent broad areas of further interest rather than an attempt to produce an encyclopaedic coverage of modern theoretical debates in psychology, which is neither possible nor appropriate here.

The Scientific Renaissance, 1450–1630 M. Boas (1962) Fontana Collins

Human Cognition: Learning, Understanding and Remembering J.D. Bransford (1979) Wadsworth USA, ISBN 0-534-00699-X

Richard III: The Maligned King A. Carson (2008) The History Press, ISBN 978-0-7524-5208-1

Facts, Fallacies and Frauds in Psychology A.M. Colman (1987) Hutchinson, ISBN 0-09-173041-4

The Descent of Mind: Psychological Perspectives on Homonid Evolution M.C. Corballis and S.E.G. Lea (1999) Oxford University Press, ISBN 0-19-852419-6

Douglas Haig, 1861–1928 G. DeGroot (1988) Unwin Hyman Ltd London, ISBN 0-04-440192-2

On the Psychology of Military Incompetence N.F. Dixon (1976) Pimlico London, ISBN 0-7126-5889-0

Our Own Worst Enemy N.F. Dixon (1987) Jonathan Cape, ISBN 0-224-02372-1

Richard III from Contemporary Chronicles, Letters and Records K. Dockray and P. Hammond, Eds (2013) Fonthill, ISBN 978-1-78155-313-8

Rebel With a Cause H.J. Eysenck (1990) WH Allen, ISBN 1-85227-162-0

Historical and Philosophical Foundations of Psychology M. Farrell (2014) Cambridge University Press, ISBN 978-1-107-00599-0

The Authoritarian Personality T.W. Adorno, E. Frenkel-Brunswik, D.J. Levinson, R. Nevitt Sanford et al (1950) Harper and Bros USA

Understanding Driving. Applying cognitive psychology to a complex everyday task. J.A. Groeger (2000) The Psychology Press, ISBN 0-415-18752-4

Richard III and the Murder in the Tower P. Hancock (2011) The History Press UK, ISBN 978-0-7524-5797-0

Richard III: A Study of Service R. Horrox (1989) Cambridge University Press, ISBN 0-521-33428-4

Victims of groupthink: A psychological study of foreign-policy decisions and fiascoes I.L. Janis (1972) Houghton Mifflin

30-Second Psychology C. Jarrett (2011) Ivy Press, ISBN 978-1-84831-261-6

Churchill R. Jenkins (2001) Pan London, ISBN 0330-48805-8

Psychology and Common Sense R.B. Joynson (1974) Routledge and Kegan Paul, ISBN 0-7100-7827-7

The Face of Battle J. Keegan (1976) Jonathan Cape London, ISBN 0-224-01232-0

Richard the Third P.M. Kendall (1955) WW Norton & Co London, ISBN 0-393-00785-5

The Bones of a King: Richard III Rediscovered M. Kennedy and L. Foxhall, Eds (2015) Wiley and Sons, Chichester, ISBN 9781118783146

The Search for Richard III: The King's Grave P. Langley and M. Jones (2013) John Murray, ISBN 978-1-84854-890-9

The Man Himself. Richard III – A psychological portrait M.W. Lansdale and J. Boon (2013) *The Ricardian,* March 2013, ISSN 0308-4337

Culture and Systems of Thought: Holistic Versus Analytic Cognition R. Nisbett, K. Peng, I. Choi and A. Norenzayan, *Psychological Review* 108 (2001) pp 291–310

Good King Richard? An Account of Richard III and his Reputation J. Potter (1983) Constable, ISBN 0-09-468840-0

Richard III C. Ross (1999) Yale University Press, ISBN 0-300-07979-6

The Daughter of Time J. Tey (1951) Random Books London, ISBN 9780099536826